Mind Over Emotions

How to Mentally Control Your Feelings

Les Carter

BAKER BOOK HOUSE
Grand Rapids, Michigan 49506

ISBN: 0-8010-2504-4

Sixth printing, July 1989

Library of Congress
Card Catalog Number: 84-73552

Unless indicated otherwise, Scripture references are from The New American Standard Bible ©
The Lockman Foundation 1960, 1962, 1963, 1968, 1971, 1973, 1975, 1977.

Printed in the United States of America

To my Parents,
Ed and Anne Carter
with Love and Gratitude

Contents

Mind Over . . .

Preface

All people are emotional. Some display their feelings openly, while others hide them. Yet we all experience them in our own way.

In addition, all people are sinful. Some have a reasonable control over their sin nature; others sin flagrantly. No one is completely immune to sin.

When we combine these two facts (all people are emotional and all people are sinful), we arrive at the conclusion that all of us will handle our feelings imperfectly. Note that emotions themselves are not sinful; our ways of dealing with them often reflect our sinfulness. The question is: How we can hold our imperfect emotional nature in check?

A woman once told me, "I try hard to control them but my emotions always seem to get the best of me. I promise myself that I'll get a grip on them, but something usually snaps. I wish I didn't have so many struggles with my feelings!"

Every day I talk with people who have emotional difficulties. Individuals are unique in the way they exhibit their emotionality. Some people have an explosive and dramatic way of showing their feelings. Whether it is anger or guilt or anxiety, these people seem to let anyone and everyone in on what is happening inside. On the other hand, I see many people who hold their feelings in so carefully that they appear stonefaced to those who know them best. Such persons are no less emotional than the more open people; they just handle things differently.

All of these individuals have a common desire to change. They are people who are seeking avenues to a new life. Tired of a topsy-turvy lifestyle controlled by uncomfortable moods, they want to be grounded in something steady. They want to feel content with who they are and with their abilities to handle interpersonal relations appropriately.

Some people have problems that would be classified as severe, while others have more ordinary struggles. But regardless of the type or severity of the emotional problem at hand, my desire is to help them discover that there is only one road to emotional maturity, the road of Christ-centered mental control.

Romans 12:2 reads: "Do not be conformed to this world, but be transformed by the renewing of your mind." These words were written over 1900 years ago by the apostle Paul to a people who struggled in every way due to the pressures of living in an ungodly world. The Roman people were exposed to a self-centered, God-forsaking pattern of living that would sweep individuals away to utter ruin in their personal lives. In his letter to them, Paul was explaining that there is a way to gain a sense of lasting stability through Jesus Christ. The message was clear: If you want to have a transformed life you can do it by renewing your mind, by allowing the Holy Spirit to work in your heart and life. This truth is still pertinent today. The important commandment for all of us is to "love the Lord your God with all your heart and with all your soul and with all your mind. And a second like it is this: You shall love your neighbor as yourself" (Matt. 22:37, 39).

We can take this to mean that if a person is to take charge of his emotional self, he can do it by becoming mentally rooted in the absolute truth of the Scripture. We are told: "As he thinks within himself, so is he" (Prov. 23:7). We all need the fixed, solid principles of the Bible to direct our lives in a meaningful manner. God's word provides a reliable, unshakable foundation for our very shakable emotional natures.

Notice what can happen when a person's emotional nature is left unrestrained. Emotions are such that one troublesome feeling can have a domino effect on other feelings. For example, a person who nurses worry may be led to feel disillusioned, which could lead to fits of impatience and anger, which could lead to struggles with guilt, then depression, then loneliness, and so on. When the emotional nature is controlled by Christian reasoning, these problems may surface but do not dominate one's life.

You can place your mind over your emotions. This will be accomplished when you follow a three-fold process.

1. Thoroughly understand the functions of each emotion. Do you ever pause to think about the reasons God has allowed us to have various emotional reactions? It is my goal to challenge you to do more than just feel your emotions. I would like you to understand them.

Generally speaking, what purpose do your emotions serve? Think first of the positive emotions (joy, peace, love, happiness) as being given to you by a benevolent God who wishes you to experience contentment and satisfaction as you move about in your daily life. These positive emotions are to life as spices are to food. Experienced in a proper amount, they add flavor and zest. Our Creator gave you these emotions so you can have an experiential understanding of His merciful, gracious nature.

But what about the more "negative" emotions, the ones that cause difficulty and problems? Many of these emotions will be explored in the following chapters. Does God really want you to experience them? Think of it this way: Because you are a sinner, there will be times when you inevitably will conduct yourself in ways that are not pleasing to God. You need inner "steering mechanisms" to keep you on track. Consequently, God has placed within you the various "negative" emotions as "warning flags" which indicate that you need to take inventory of your thoughts, behaviors, and attitudes.

For example, we will explore how envy indicates that an individual has placed too much emphasis on the rewards and gains experienced by someone else. So as we recognize persistent feelings of envy, we can view this emotion as being a signal indicating that priorities need to be examined. Likewise, we will look at how anger is tied to our list of priorities. And we will notice that if we experience anger too often, we can interpret the emotion as a signal indicating a need to explore how insecurities are influencing our manner of standing up for our convictions.

With each emotional experience, we can learn to train ourselves to become psychologically attuned to the message it is emitting. By understanding the function and purpose of the emotion, we will be one step further in the understanding of ourselves.

2. Be keenly aware of the behaviors and attitudes that accompany each emotion. It has always been interesting for me to observe how so many people have limited their understanding of their emotions by accepting certain stereotypes about each emotion. For example, we usually think of a proud person as being haughty and arrogant. But have you ever thought of a hesitant, worrying person as one who has struggles with pride? Likewise, we tend to think of loneliness as being an emotion experienced chiefly by the socially isolated person without realizing that the glib conversationalist is also prone to it.

There is no one way that a particular emotion will manifest itself. We are all different in the way we expose and handle our feelings. Consequently, as we examine each of the emotions in the book, we will explore the variety of behavioral indicators that point to the presence of that emotion. It is important for each of us to know our unique patterns of displaying our emotions because self-awareness is a key in making the proper moves to keep the emotions under proper control.

3. Commit your emotional nature to God. Finally, in order to gain mental control over your emotions, it will be important to integrate the teachings from God's word into your life. God is not silent regarding the ways you can handle your emotions. From Scripture you can gain insights for dealing with guilt, worry, anger, and all other emotions.

As we comprehend the teachings of Scripture regarding our emotions, we will arrive at the conclusion that the most important step a person can make toward establishing emotional stability is to commit one's life to God through Jesus Christ. This is done by humbly admitting one's sins and inadequacies to God, and then declaring the need for a Savior to bring oneself into a right fellowship with God. Jesus Christ is the only one who can restore a person to wholeness because He is the only one who has successfully conquered sin and death. When we claim Him as Savior and Lord, we are also claiming His strength which enables us to live lives of composure and stability.

We are told that once Jesus becomes our Savior, the Holy Spirit is sent to us to give us His eternal presence and guidance. (Read John 16:7–15.) When we willfully respond to the presence of the Holy Spirit, we are assured that we will be blessed with His fruit: love, joy, patience, kindness, goodness, faithfulness, gentleness, and self-control. (See Galatians 5:22–23.) The fruit of the Holy Spirit will balance our tendency to nurture our problematic emotions.

Notice one major thought: God has already supplied all things necessary to give individuals peace and composure. He has given us a mind, the ability to have insights to understand the purpose of the emotions. He has given us consequences, both positive and negative, to steer us in our behaviors. And He has given us the strength and guidance of His Holy Spirit. The key, then, is for each of us to mentally acknowledge the leadership God gives us, yielding ourselves to His will. So, then, let us use our minds to control our emotions, to offer them in service to our Lord.

1

Anger

Who me? Angry? You must be kidding. Oh sure, I get frustrated or irritated from time to time, but never angry."

It never ceases to amaze me how people will go to great lengths to avoid admitting the extent of their anger. (I can't be too accusatory, though, because sometimes I'm part of this crowd). Anger has a nasty reputation, so naturally most of us are a bit hesitant to acknowledge its presence in our lives. Instead, we tend to dance around the issue. That is, we will admit to being annoyed, perturbed, aggravated, peeved, hurt, or frustrated; but seldom will we actually admit to being angry.

Yet when the truth is exposed, there is a shadow of anger in each of the words just mentioned. The anger may not be blatant, but it is there nonetheless. We all have anger. This is simply a fact. Therefore it is prudent for us to discover how to use it positively, and how to avoid the wrong use of it.

Case Study

Randall, now in his late thirties, had a history of troubled relationships in both his social and family life. When I suggested that we should examine his style of handling his anger, he flinched. Proudly, he maintained that he virtually never yelled or even spoke firmly. So (he supposed) this meant that anger was not his problem. However, as we explored the subject, we discussed how Randall had a tendency to hold grudges when people behaved contrary to his liking. He had a habit of judgmentally evaluating those who were in his presence. While he was not the type to openly attack others, he was prone to subtle sarcasm and to critical second-guessing. In addition, Randall would rarely exchange verbal blows in arguments; rather, he was a frequent user of the silent treatment (thereby being a "punishing" communicator). As time went on Randall began to understand that while he was not a person who had a problem with a boisterous, slashing style of anger, the anger was still exhibited. He realized his need to recognize his tricky, hidden means of expressing anger.

It is important to note that anger is not necessarily a negative emotion. Not at all. In fact, anger can have a very positive function. It is the way anger is expressed that makes it either a positive or negative force. The fact that anger has been severely abused by most of us gives us a powerful motivation to understand it so that we learn to use it properly.

Anger *is the emotional response that is tied to one's psychological sense of self-preservation. Anger involves standing up for one's sense of convictions and one's sense of self-worth. When an individual feels angry he is being an advocate for himself and his beliefs.*

Think of the times when your anger (frustration, irritation, annoyance) is aroused. Usually people become angry when they feel ignored, insulted, unduly criticized, abandoned, controlled, or misunderstood. Anger communicates: "Hey, notice me! Notice my needs! Please, treat me right!"

Rarely does a person feel angry when he is complimented or when people treat him fairly. Notice that anger results from a remark or event that violates yourself or one of your beliefs. This is why anger is defined as a self-preserving mechanism. When we see anger as being intricately interwoven with one's sense of personal beliefs and self-worth, it becomes apparent that anger is a positive emotion. At its core, anger is the emotion that seeks to correct wrongs.

But here is the catch: while anger was meant to have a positive function, we tend to misuse it most of the time. Some people express anger in a destructive manner 90–95 percent of the times they use it. No wonder that anger has a bad reputation.

In general, there are two basic ways that anger is expressed: aggressive and assertive. In each episode of anger the individual is attempting to take a stand for himself or for his convictions, but with differing results.

Aggressive Anger

An individual who uses aggressive anger is attempting to make a stand for his personal worth or convictions without giving due consideration to the other persons involved. Consequently, aggressive anger tends to have an abrasive, insensitive, manner and is usually accompanied by judgmental, negative overtones. And what is worse, aggressive anger tends to remain perpetually unresolved. Because it is offensive in nature, it rarely "hits home" with the other person, and the desired result rarely occurs.

Case Study

Phyllis learned the hard way that aggressive anger often serves only to encourage more aggressive anger. She was the kind of person who would become indignant when family members or friends would violate one of her convictions. For example, when her husband came home late from work, she would berate him for being an insensitive, irresponsible family man. But because of this abrasive manner of expression, she rarely received the desired response from him. What would result? You guessed it: more anger. It seemed that the more aggressive Phyllis was in her communication, the easier it became to be aggressive the next time. Obviously, Phyllis needed to express her anger in a more positive, less threatening way.

When we think of aggressive anger, we tend to pinpoint the loud, obnoxious style of nagging or ranting and raving. This loud type of anger does qualify as aggressive anger. But there are also more subtle ways of being aggressive (angry and insensitive). The following behaviors qualify as aggressive anger.

Loud, Obnoxious Behavior

The most obvious style of aggressive anger is blustery and forceful. A person who uses this style of anger definitely desires to take a stance for a specific conviction. However, the person who is the object of this anger usually suffers greatly. Behaviors in this category include: yelling, loud cursing, finger pointing, throwing objects, furiously pacing the floor, name calling, and temper outbursts.

Open, Cutting Behavior

This prevalent, toned-down style of being aggressive is not necessarily accompanied by flailing the arms or by piercing screams, but it still fits the aggressive definition because it is not considerate of the needs of other people. Behaviors in this category include sarcasm, critical thoughts and words, bossiness, cornering questions, blaming, gossip, open insults, complaining, and whining.

Passive Aggressive Behavior

This type of aggressive anger is the most subtle and perhaps the most difficult to handle. The individual is very slyly communicating anger while not "owning up" to it. Behaviors in this category include the silent treatment, holding grudges, social withdrawal, deliberate ignoring, cold and icy glares, laziness, procrastination, giving half-hearted efforts, chronic forgetfulness, and chronic tardiness.

In each of these forms of aggressive anger it is obvious how they serve the function of helping a person take a stance for a personal conviction. However, it is also clear that each of these behaviors sabotages constructive interpersonal relations. If a person resorts to aggressive behavior, that is an indication that a more productive style of anger is necessary. Using assertive anger can meet that need.

Assertive Anger

An individual who uses assertive anger is attempting to make a stand for his personal convictions or self-worth while at the same time considering the needs of other persons involved. It is natural and legitimate for an individual to have a desire to see that his most basic personal needs are met. This is why Scripture tells us to "be angry and yet do not sin; do not let the sun go down on your anger" (Eph. 4:26). That is, there are times when responsible behavior demands that we take a stand for our convictions.

While it is important to note that assertive anger can be a responsible move, it is also wise to consider that the Bible teaches us to be conservative in its use. James 1:19 states: "But let everyone be quick to hear, slow to speak, and slow to anger." In other words, do not be guilty of overdoing a good thing.

Case Study

Sarah had a habit of using passive-aggressive anger as the major means of taking a stand for herself. She deliberately ignored the person she was angry with. As we explored how this style of anger seemed to lead to many bouts with unending frustration, we determined that a more open, assertive style of anger was needed. However, a couple of weeks later when I talked again with Sarah it became apparent to me that she had overstepped her limits. That is, she was making clear-cut stands for her convictions, but she was not exercising a keen sensitivity to other people's needs. Sarah needed to learn that assertiveness always involves tact and diplomacy.

We need a sense of caution as we examine the different ways of being assertively angry. The following behaviors could be classified as assertive anger. (These actions may not seem to be angry behaviors. But that is due to the fact that we are conditioned to think of anger as a negative, vile emotion.)

Publicly Stating Your Beliefs and Opinions

Since anger is tied to your sense of conviction, it is only natural that assertive anger would include stating your opinions. This can be a positive way of declaring yourself while remaining sensitive to the feelings of others.

Saying No When Necessary

We all encounter circumstances which tax us to the limit. Consequently, in our efforts toward self-preservation there are times when our responsibility to ourselves and others requires that we relinquish some tasks. After all, people who say yes to too many requests can eventually become so worn out that they are good to no one.

Setting Boundaries

Another way of being responsible in anger is to let your limits be known. We all have legitimate limitations, so we might as well be honest. For example, an office worker can state to a colleague: "I can help you with your project for the next thirty minutes, but then I'll have to get back to other matters."

Openly Seeking to Clarify Issues

Most of us can recall being in meetings or having family discussions that resulted in confusion because people didn't completely understand each other. Consequently, there are times to seek clarification in communication. This is a style of assertiveness since it involves the desire to take care of one's personal needs.

Asking for Favors

Assertiveness can come in the form of asking others to give you help. Note how this fits the definition of anger because by asking for help you are standing for your personal needs and convictions and at the same time you are avoiding frustration.

As you survey the behaviors listed as assertive anger you will detect in them a distinct lack of harshness or abrasiveness. Consequently, these behaviors hardly seem to be anger. Yet, in each instance, you are being an advocate for yourself. You can speculate that if you fail to act assertively when such action is called for, you are increasing the possibility for aggressiveness. For example, if you fail to set a responsible limit when your spouse asks you to do extra chores, you will probably feel resentment or irritation building inside yourself. So by being properly assertive, you could actually avoid later aggression.

Why Anger Gets Out of Hand

Anger is an easily abused emotion. In fact, it is most frequently used in a destructive manner. We all know how easily anger can become explosive and how easily it can linger underground. Before we discuss ways to mentally control anger, it would be helpful to examine some of the reasons why anger tends to indwell people to an extreme.

Need for Affirmation

All humans are needy; no individual is completely self-sufficient. It is neither possible nor desirable for a person to get to the position in life where he or she needs no one. It is normal for each of us to desire the strokes or affirmation that are a part of human relations. However, a person who uses aggressive anger is going too far in the realm of personal neediness.

Remember the function of anger: to take a stance for one's needs and convictions. A person who is overusing his anger is thereby overstating his needs. His needs have become wants. He is in effect communicating: "I'm unable to conduct myself properly if you don't agree to my wants." He is looking too intently for a sign that says: "You're okay. I can see things from your point of view."

Case Study

Chester thought he was an extremely independent person who never suffered from feelings of neediness. But Chester had a bad temper. As a construction supervisor, he easily became irate when a job was done poorly or slowly. And at home, he regularly griped about how his wife and kids didn't treat him with respect. In a technical sense, Chester's anger was justified. After all, his anger caused him to take a stand for himself. However, because Chester's anger easily became aggressive, it was apparent that he had an inward insecurity which surfaced when his workers or family members didn't give him a fair shake. He craved affirmation. With anger Chester was trying to force others to prove that they thought of him as a significant person.

The danger of looking too intently to other people for affirmation of self is readily apparent. Since we are imperfect people, flaws in our interpersonal interactions are guaranteed and normal. Therefore, it is best to moderate our desires to receive pats on the back from people. No human can make us feel good at all times. Our fullest sense of affirmation comes from our Creator, God Himself.

Inner Tunnel Vision

When a person has the tendency to be so intent in wanting his needs to be met that nothing else matters, anger can be a self-centered problem. That is, the individual has concern for no one or nothing except his own feelings and his own point of view.

Case Study

Cherrie was prone toward the passive-aggressive behavior of holding inward resentments. When a friend or family member slighted her, she could carry a grudge for weeks. Cherrie was the kind of person who would speculate in her mind about what could happen to bring her a sense of satisfaction. Over and over she would think, "Why can't they just understand what I want?" Or she would constantly think, "I know I could become calm if we could just come to a comfortable agreement." Her problem was that she would so stubbornly hold on to her thoughts that no solution short of total perfection would satisfy her anger. She saw no one else's point of view.

Most angry people would agree that there are usually two sides to any argument. Yet because of personal insecurities or chronic mistrust of others, angry people usually exhibit an unwillingness to survey all sides of an issue until their needs are satisfactorily resolved. While the anger itself may be a correct reaction, it becomes a negative emotion because of the tendency to balk until one's own needs are met.

Striving for Superiority

Anger most frequently occurs when a person feels that he has been placed in an inferior position. In fact, when we are angry, we often use phrases that indicate a worthless feeling: "Don't talk down to me" or "I hate being treated like a nobody." Anger quite often is the response of one who is trying to be an advocate for self, to build himself up.

It is healthy to maneuver ourselves to a position of being co-equal (assertive anger). After all, God has made us all with equal worth and value. However, when a person uses aggressive anger, he is seeking to go from a one-down position to a one-up position. Or, to put it in other words, aggressive anger seeks to establish a position of superiority.

This striving for superiority is obvious in the blatant expressions of aggression, such as shouting. Superiority is also the goal (however, more subtle) when passive-aggressive behavior, such as the silent treatment, is used. With either behavior the angry person is trying to put the other person in his place.

As an example, Anita seemed to be forever frustrated because her husband, Phil, was such a domineering man. She felt as if she was the spouse who was permanently assigned the low-position on the totem pole. This was not satisfactory to her, so she decided to get even. (Actually when we say we want to get even, we really mean we want to establish superiority.)

Anita decided to resist whenever Phil became demanding. She used various resistance methods. She would let him fix his own meals if he criticized her early in the day, she would deliberately withhold sex, and she would tauntingly point out his failings and weaknesses. Inwardly she thought, "I'll just let him see what it's like to have a taste of his own medicine."

Whether a person is blunt (as Anita was) or subtle in trying to gain superiority, it virtually never works. You see, when one person establishes a superior position, someone else must necessarily take the inferior position. And since we all dislike the position of inferiority, each of us is likely to play his own games to grab the one-up position. A never-ending "see-saw" effect occurs.

Shaky Self-Image

Errant anger begins with a troubled self-image. Since the self-image is the bedrock foundation on which all emotions are based, a person who is struggling with who he is will be easily angered.

In a group therapy session bad-tempered Sam proudly proclaimed: "I may have a couple of problems, but one problem I don't have is my self-image." A perceptive young woman spoke up and said: "If you feel so good about yourself, then why do you get so bent out of shape when someone does something you don't like?" Sam didn't have an answer. Secretly, he knew she was on target.

Anger itself is not an indication of a self-image problem. In fact, a person with a healthy self-image will recognize that there are times when it is appropriate and responsible to be assertively angry. It is when the anger goes to the extremes of being openly hostile or passively controlling that struggles with self-image are indicated.

The individual who uses aggressive anger is indicating an unhealthy sensitivity to the flaws of others, which stems from his need to have everything in its place in order to protect a fragile ego. The person who is excessively angry is saying, "Notice my needs!" (which is fine). But he is holding so tightly to his needs that in effect he is communicating, "I'll lose my stability if things don't go according to my plans." The inner personal struggle is clear.

How to Control Anger

Of all troublesome emotions, anger tends to be the most volatile and has the most potential for damaging one's inner stability and outer relations. It is vital to control this emotion.

Preserving Yourself Without Being Selfish

Anger is the emotion most closely connected with one's sense of self-preservation. God has given each individual an inner desire to be taken care of and to be treated properly. So it is normal when an individual responds to the emotional urge to stand up for himself. But we have a characteristic that makes this drive for self-preservation potentially dangerous: selfishness. Only when selfishness is throttled can self-preservation be pursued in the responsible fashion.

Too many people have assumed that there is no difference between self-preservation and selfishness. (Usually these are people who were taught to never feel angry.) These folks assume it is wrong to do things for themselves. So they condemn any use of anger altogether. This false assumption drives anger underground.

A first step toward gaining control over anger is to consider moderate self-preservation as an act of responsibility. Recognize that when you feel relatively satisfied that your needs are being fulfilled, other people will benefit as much as you.

Case Study

Becky had once been prone to fits of frustration because her family members seemed to be oblivious to her emotional needs. At times they could be downright rude. Realizing that her tendency to hold her feelings inward was counterproductive, she decided to politely, but firmly tell each intruding family member how they could help to make a more pleasant atmosphere at home. She accomplished two things: she became a positive influence in her family, and she felt relieved that her personal needs could be met. She did this without an air of self-centeredness.

Distinguishing Assertiveness from Bitterness

Two Bible verses teach us a delicate lesson about anger.

Ephesians 4:26 says: "Be angry, and yet do not sin; do not let the sun go down on your anger."

Then Ephesians 4:31 states: "Let all bitterness and wrath and anger and clamor and slander be put away from you, along with all malice."

What we have in this seeming contradiction is a biblical distinction between assertive and aggressive anger. The Bible tells us to experience anger when it is morally necessary, but to keep anger brief so it won't grow into the bitterness that ultimately leads to hate.

Bitter anger is never productive and it is to be avoided at all costs. Bitterness is beneath the varying characteristics of aggressive anger such as explosiveness, sarcasm, or undue criticism. When a person learns to distinguish the difference between assertiveness and bitterness, he will find the ability to control anger. He can deliberately choose to avoid actions that would communicate bitterness.

Focusing Anger on Essentials Only

A major reason that anger has a negative reputation is that it is often wasted on nonessential matters. For example, some people get completely irrational because a meaningless TV program has been interrupted. Others become irate because of an innocent or minor mistake made by a spouse or a child. The expression of anger is inconsistent with the size of the problem. If the consequences of such anger weren't so grave, we could become quite amused over their outbursts.

What causes people to let their anger fly?

To gain control over anger, ask yourself: "Will it help matters if I take a firm stance at this point?" Or, "Do I need to make this criticism?" When the answer is yes, then proceed carefully. If you cannot honestly determine that the anger will serve a useful function, dismiss it.

Learning to Dismiss Anger

Although anger cannot be shut off instantly like a water faucet, it is possible to gain enough control over anger to determine the degree and direction of it. Anger is a choice; it does not have to be a dominant emotion in our lives. We can choose to use it carefully and considerately.

There are times when even assertive anger can cause harm, such as when the timing is poor, or the person listening to the anger fails to grasp what we are trying to communicate. These are the times when it is best to go to Plan B: drop the anger altogether.

Granted, it's hard to drop anger, particularly when you feel very right about it. But when assertive anger serves no useful function, you can decide that your anger must leave. When you have a mind-set that desires to do whatever is constructive, with dogged determination you can make choices about how much anger you will allow in your behavior patterns.

Case Study

For years Ed had been working to control his anger. He realized the need to weed out his old aggressive behaviors and to find ways to be properly assertive. He was truly committed to self-improvement in this area of his life. But Ed didn't know what to do when people failed to respond positively to his new-found assertiveness.

For example, there were times when he felt he was offering constructive criticism to his wife. Instead of responding in a style of openness, she would cry. Even though Ed was technically correct in his assertiveness, he had to consider the alternative of dropping his anger altogether. His anger was not wrong, but it was not helpful, either. Dismissing his untimely anger became one of Ed's most challenging tasks.

The key to being able to dismiss anger is having the self-confidence to withstand life's imperfections. Such a person doesn't have to have perfection before he can feel stable. His self-image is intact; he draws stability from within himself, based on his relationship with God.

How to Handle Other People's Anger

Anger usually tends to be a two-way emotion. That is, it involves a minimum of two people: oneself and a partner. In order to have a steady hand on anger, it is helpful to know what to do with someone else's anger as well as one's own.

When people ask me what they should do when someone else (spouse, roommate, sibling, child, co-worker, acquaintance) becomes angry, my first response is to have that person examine his attitudes about the anger of the other person. Usually I find that the individual is highly threatened when another person becomes angry. This is dangerous since it usually leads to a very defensive and unhelpful response to the anger.

Case Study

Alice was a friendly woman who could be described as a harmonizer. She had the knack of putting people at ease and was skilled in being a "social diplomat." Alice was at her very best when she was able to create an atmosphere of calm in her interpersonal surroundings.

But this strength often backfired in her family setting. Alice's husband and two teenage sons were not always responsive to her efforts to create a composed, calm climate at home. They were prone to be volatile in their emotions, particularly anger. Sixteen-year-old, Mark would often respond rudely to Alice's mild suggestions about social courtesies. He would sarcastically tell her that her name wasn't "Dear Abby" and he hadn't asked for her advice. Her husband, Dwayne, was usually not as biting as Mark in his use of anger, but Dwayne tended to be bossy and overly critical.

This often threw Alice into moods of disillusionment. For years, she had taken pride in her control of anger. She never yelled and rarely exchanged sharp words with her family. And she wasn't the type to respond to another person's sarcasm with snide remarks of her own. Yet while she had mastered her own anger, she still had to learn what to do with other people's anger.

Alice came to my counseling office because she feared she was blind to potential errors she was making in her relationships. First, we focused on her responses to her husband's or sons' anger. Alice very readily admitted that she became uneasy and tense with their anger and viewed their emotions as being blatant hindrances to her goal of composure. Then we discussed how this reaction caused her to do the very thing she wished to avoid. She would actually help escalate the anger level by believing that the best response to someone else's anger was no response. Presumably this would give the anger a chance to die down. What she failed to realize was that her family members (particularly Dwayne) interpreted her reaction as a rejection of them, which only increased their anger. As Alice and I discussed her need to revamp her style of responding to another person's anger, we reviewed the suggestions given below.

Preventing Someone Else's Weaknesses from Threatening You

No question about it, it is often uncomfortable being on the receiving end of another person's bad mood. But it's not the end of the earth. Rather than becoming inwardly shaken, remind yourself that since all of us are sinful people who have moments during which we handle ourselves in a less-than-exemplary manner. Mistakes, even bad ones, are part of life.

Trying to Solve Problems in the Open

Responding to another person's anger with silence usually doesn't work. Neither do arguments and counterattacks. Rather, sit down with the angry person when calmness returns, and discuss what could be done the next time anger erupts. Seek solutions. Draw the individuals involved into the resolution of their own anger. Map out a game plan to give guidelines for handling an angry situation.

Holding Firmly to Your Strength in God

When another person is angry, it does not mean that you must latch on to instant feelings of insecurity. Rather, can remind yourself that you have given your personal stability over to God. Even when you are being insulted or "chewed out" or criticized, you can maintain your "cool" because you are dependent on God, not humans, for your ultimate feeling of security. Admittedly, this is easier said than done, but it is possible.

Learning to Say "You're Right"

If someone is inappropriately angry with you, he or she is usually seeking emotional support or approval, so use the opportunity to give it. Get beyond your immediate instinct to defend yourself. Determine the key point the angry person is trying to make, and openly make note of it. Seek an opportunity to show that you hear and understand what is being said. Break down the barriers of poor communication. Set an example worthy to be followed.

As you learn how to respond both to your own anger and to the anger of another person, you will find anger to be a manageable emotion. Not only can you discover that anger is not always an enemy, you may also see that anger can offer new opportunities for better interpersonal relationships.

Questions for Further Thought

What am I trying to accomplish when I became angry? Am I trying to take a stand for my convictions, or am I trying to make people squirm?

What is my usual style of anger? In particular, which aggressive behaviors do to I need to avoid?

In what way does my anger reflect my self-image? Am I confident and loving, or do I seek to establish superiority?

Can I handle the fact that the world around me will present problems? Or do I become threatened if another person shows a weakness?

2

Defensiveness

I overheard this husband-and-wife conversation in a department store. It went something like this:

H: "Why is it that you're so eager to blow our money? You always want more!"

W: "What do you mean *our* money? I feel like a little kid who has to beg for every last penny."

H: If you showed that you could be more responsible, I might cut you some slack. But you'll never learn."

W: "I don't know why I even bother talking to you. You never listen."

With this the wife stormed out of the store and headed for the car, her husband close behind. I knew that this couple was in for a long, rotten day. Their stubbornness was at a high peak and each was cornered into feelings of defensiveness. As one responded in a defensive manner, the other followed suit. My guess is that these two people had already had too much experience with defensiveness.

Everyone experiences the feeling of resistance in interpersonal relationships. We have had those moments when we felt provoked into defending our egos, even if it meant engaging in less-than-desirable behavior patterns. At times even the most open and agreeable people feel the need to protect themselves from the strains of perceived threats. Occasionally, defensiveness is useful. After all, this world can provide some very offensive experiences. But problems arise when defensiveness becomes deeply engrained in one's personality.

Defensiveness *is a person's resistance to personal frustration and interpersonal conflict, a protective measure which shields oneself from anxiety due to a perceived threat.*

While defensiveness is meant to relieve anxiety, it usually serves the opposite function. That is, an individual may temporarily postpone outer conflict by defensive behaviors, but in the long run defensiveness actually creates greater problems because frequently it tends to be accompanied by stubbornness and manipulative communication styles.

Often defensiveness is subconscious, sneaking up on us so quickly that we are hardly aware of its presence, and leading to unhealthy levels of self-deception. This lethal emotion can cause a person to chart a course of interpersonal relating that leads straight downhill. To facilitate self-examination in this area, look at several common examples of behaviors caused by feelings of defensiveness.

Defensive Behaviors

Denying Unpleasant Realities

Many times people can feel so uncomfortable about their flawed behaviors and feelings that they choose to ignore their presence. This is usually subconscious. Denial is one of the most often used defensive behaviors. For example, a teenaged daughter whines to her mother, "Mom, you're so strict with me. I don't think you want me to make any major decisions." The mother replies, "That's not true. I always let you make your own decisions." There is no acknowledgment that the daughter may have a legitimate perception. Mother denies any personal flaw.

Tuning Out Other People

There are times when individuals feel reluctant to communicate openly because they fear becoming involved in a relationship. Effort is involved in any satisfying interaction and we differ in our levels of willingness to work. An easy way of avoiding potential conflict or frustration is to tune out. To illustrate, picture a husband who responds to his wife's questions by passively stating: "Sure, Honey, whatever you think."

Transferring Blame

A classic example of defensiveness is the individual who continually seeks someone else to blame for life's problems. Pointing the accusing finger elsewhere, relieves him of the burden of problem solving.

"Boomeranging"

Most of us do not like to be confronted with our weaknesses and have an instinctive inclination to protect ourselves when the subject of a personal flaw arises. We quickly maneuver to take the focus off self and boomerang it to the confronting individual. For example, when a wife suggests to her husband that he should help her more in taking care of the kids on the weekend, he retorts: "Well, that's gratitude for you. I think you'd better consider how well I treat this family. Remember how lucky you are before you criticize me." He has succeeded in taking the focus off himself and throwing it back to his wife.

Taking the Offensive

In football the theory is that the best defense is a good offense; in relationships the same idea often holds true. Some people resist any intrusion into their feelings or thoughts. These people especially avoid situations which might reveal their insecurities or weaknesses. Consequently, they defend themselves by putting other people on the hot seat, using excessive criticism and bossiness to accomplish their purpose.

Rationalizing

Do you know what it is like to talk with someone who has an air-tight explanation for virtually everything? Such an individual intellectualizes (rationalizes) personal issues so that real feelings and personal issues are completely avoided. For example, someone with a problem temper explains that he could probably get a grip on his moodiness if only the stresses of work and home would ease. He says: "I'm a basically calm person, but things just aren't very steady right now."

Projecting

Since we have faults that we would rather not face up to, it is sometimes easier to pretend they don't exist. It becomes so simple to see those repressed faults in someone else. Projection occurs when an individual attributes his repressed flaws to someone else as a means of sidestepping personal responsibility. For example, a critical person may say: "You know, it really bugs me about the way Joe seems to criticize so much. Why does he think he has the right to be so finicky?"

Using Sarcasm

Another behavior that results from defensive feelings is sarcasm. In an effort to disguise anger that we prefer not to own up to, or to vent it in a less threatening mode, we choose to make critical jokes about others or even about oneself. For example, a woman who is irritated by her friend's over-talkative nature might say: "Joan we haven't heard from you all day, what's on your mind?"

Fantasizing

When we want to avoid accepting unwanted truths, we sometimes use a fantasy-thinking process. Some people fool themselves into believing in idealistic notions in spite of evidence to the contrary. For example, for months a woman, whose husband left her to marry someone else, said to her friends: "I know that God is not going to let him marry that woman. My husband will return to me." She was not willing to accept the fact that sometimes God reluctantly permits such sins.

People with fragile egos cannot face personal problems. They prefer to delude themselves into believing that their life is in complete and perfect order. This too is a means of defensive self-protection. I recall a man who repeatedly stated: "If my life was any better I don't think I could stand the thrill of it all." However, I knew of his inward turmoil because his two grown sons had completely severed relations with him.

Holding Stubbornly to Opinions

Another way to defend oneself and to resist conflict is to be so firm in one's beliefs that no allowance is made for someone else's desires or behavior. Strongly opinionated persons may temporarily defer an anxiety, but eventually they encounter increased frustrations. The father who believes in the old rule, "Children should be seen and not heard," may succeed for several years in running a tight ship, only to have his kids rebel when they reach the teen years.

Using Passive-Aggressive Techniques

In an effort to avoid confrontation and to protect themselves, some people use deliberate silence or procrastination. By using such passive-aggressive behaviors, these people can accomplish two acts at once: they express their feelings of frustration and anger but do not expose their vulnerability.

Why People Feel Defensive

As we explore our defensive feelings and their resultant behaviors, we are motivated to understand better why we do what we do. That is a crucial first step in gaining control of our emotions. Now we will examine some explanations of why people feel defensive.

The Need to Maintain Self-Esteem

When you try to understand your defensive emotions, the first question is: "What am I defending?" Virtually always the answer will be: "I'm defending myself." The most valuable resource an individual has is his own inner sense of security or self-esteem. Being created in the image of God, each person is born with an inner sense of self-worth and a self-protective mechanism that prompts him to do everything possible to be treated in a worthy manner. But since a defensive person's self-esteem is shaky in the first place, he goes too far to maintain self-protection. In defensiveness there is an implicit fear of confrontation with reality. We don't like to examine the dark side of our personalities or our relationships, so we resort to the various cover-up techniques already described. By using them we can subconsciously deceive ourselves into maintaining a positive (but false) self-image.

Case Study

Murray was extremely sensitive to any hint of a criticism directed toward him. He had grown up in a very performance-oriented home and he had a high-pressure job. It seemed that his behaviors had always been under constant scrutiny, and he was tired of it. He wanted people to like him for who he was. He wanted pats on the back and confirmation of being a good guy, a completely understandable desire. But his craving for strokes was so powerful that he flinched emotionally whenever his wife made even a slight suggestion to him. Also, he often used sarcastic overtones when he talked about his boss. His sarcasm temporarily lifted him to a level of intellectual superiority (false self-esteem). Murray's defensive feelings were a direct result of his need for an "ego boost."

Fear of Being Vulnerable

Another reason people feel defensive is because it can be scary and risky to open oneself up to public examination and judgments. It is safer to just avoid exposing oneself. Also, if a person becomes open in a relationship, he might feel required to give of himself to allow the relationship to flourish and grow. We know that relationships require work and the defensive person usually prefers to avoid being drawn into an uncomfortable situation.

A lack of self-confidence is the root of this fear of vulnerability. When a person is a habitually defensive, he is in essence communicating: "I'm afraid to let you see the real me because I'm not sure I could handle it if you rejected me." Our innermost feelings about ourselves definitely influence our emotional and behavioral patterns.

Case Study

Janna frequently used the defensive maneuver of clamming up whenever she and her husband got into discussions about their marriage. She didn't think it was ever helpful for a couple to "air their dirty laundry" with each other. Her desire was to have only positive communications. Her philosophy could be summarized in the phrase: "If you can't say something nice don't say anything at all." However, the truth of the matter was that Janna could not admit a weakness without feeling terribly threatened. She had grown up with the hope that she would be as flawless as a person could be and that her relationships, especially marriage, would be purely blissful. If she ever opened herself up to personal examination she would be forced to rewrite her dream. Her defensive use of the fantasizing technique was fueled by her imbedded fear of letting herself become vulnerable.

Misguided Notions About Anger

Defensive people usually have an aversion to anger and confrontation. Often these individuals have seen how easily anger can be abused, so they label all anger as TERRIBLE. Granted, anger is an emotion that often has been mishandled, but we need not write it off completely. Gains can be made when anger is used in constructive confrontations; it can produce the exchange of helpful, positive feedback.

Case Study

Donna's defensive nature caused her to work hard to always appear happy and superfriendly. She abhorred confrontation. Her assumption was that if anger surfaced in a relationship, camaraderie was lost. She thought it was impossible to have confrontations with a friend. She tried to protect herself by her superfriendly nature. I suggested that she could learn to view confrontations as opportunities to grow and mature. We need close companions who are willing to be honest with us about our needs for improvement. Donna was not pleased with this suggestion. If she accepted the fact that anger and confrontation could be a part of a healthy relationship, she would be forced to give up some of her misguided, idealistic notions. She would also be forced to look on the dark side of life. She was not prepared to do this.

Often people have misguided notions about anger because they were not shown how to deal with anger in their formative years. Few ever had insightful discussions during the teen years regarding the nature of anger or disagreements. Consequently, it is only natural that adults assume the worst when a confrontation arises. Defensiveness is a natural reaction to bewilderment in dealing with disagreements.

Desire to Remain in Control

The opposite of defensiveness is openness. When a person is open, he recognizes that he does not have to maintain total control of his environment. A defensive person usually feels a strong need to control both himself and the opinions of others. Of course, this is impossible. But that doesn't stop some people who feel (consciously or sub-consciously) that they must have the power to call the shots in every relationship. Notice in the following case study how this obsession can undermine communications.

Case Study

Joan prided herself in being a person above reproach in most areas of life. As a wife and mother she ran a tidy, well-organized home. In her part-time job she preferred to be left alone so she could get her responsibilities done with the greatest efficiency. Her problem was that she had a hard time getting along well with people, both at home and work. Her husband was reluctant to ever offer a suggestion because it was usually followed by self-righteous rationalization of why Joan's method of handling the situation was best. Joan was very free in pointing out his errors, but she seemed to usually have an excuse handy if her husband asked her to change one of her traits. Likewise at work, she was very sensitive about any communication that even sounded negative. Sub-consciously, she reasoned that she was happy with the way she had established order in her life, and she would let no one challenge her.

It is normal to want to keep frustrations to a minimum. But the people who maintain a defensive, controlling posture too often (to the extent that it undermines relationships) are being idealistic. There is a lack of reality in their thinking and very little allowance for the natural errors that dog humanity. Such controlling people ultimately cause increased emotional difficulties (frustration, worry) for themselves. They fail to realize that the more they try to control people, the less control they actually have. A downward spiral usually occurs because controllers usually just press harder in their efforts.

Inability to Admit Weakness

Defensive people have caused tremendous frustrations in their friends, family, and co-workers because their emotional tightness prevents them from admitting weakness. Such people are often able to give feedback, but unable to receive it. One woman in my group-therapy session enjoyed playing the role of "junior therapist." She was delighted to help the other group members gain insight into their problems. (In truth, this lady really *was* helpful most of the time.) But her problem surfaced when it was her turn to tell the group about her inner struggles. She regularly fought with the temptation to sugar-coat her weaknesses as if they were really no big deal.

Many of us have lived with the delusion that weakness equals personal failure. In our success-oriented culture it is considered an oddity for someone to publicly admit a flaw. We assume that to make the right impressions, only the positive side of self should be exposed. But we are sinners and it is impossible to be right all the time.

Case Study

Richard looks back at his first forty years and shakes his head over his extremely strong feelings of defensiveness. Now he is committed to a life of openness and concern for others. But it took a lot of struggle for him to make this commitment.

When Richard was a boy, the other kids regarded him as a whiz kid. There was hardly any school assignment he couldn't readily master, few puzzles he couldn't solve. The other kids looked to him for academic help. Although Richard was well-developed in his intellectual skills, his social development was lacking. People were attracted to him mainly because of his mental ability.

Because Richard's reputation was tied to his academic prowess, he had a hard time letting others know when he felt inadequate. He quickly learned to be evasive about his weaknesses. And since he more easily intellectualized problem solving, he grew up shunning emotional matters because they couldn't always be solved with machine-like ease.

Richard describes his early married life as being disastrous. He married a woman who needed to share feelings and enjoyed intimate discussions. She was not adept at discussing facts and figures. Before long they experienced strife. Richard resisted his wife's offers to discuss emotions. Instead he made suggestions on how she could become more like him. When his wife cried and complained that she felt unloved, Richard's defensive response was a put-down. Actually, Richard found that when he reacted defensively, his wife responded with defensiveness of her own.

At work, Richard had similar problems. While he was brilliant in his field of computer science, he had regular clashes with fellow employees. His need to control others was enormous. One year he went through seven personal secretaries. Each time one left, he explained how it was her fault. He became cynical and sarcastic about working women.

Richard's problems with defensiveness continued unabated for years until he was hit with a jolt from out of the blue. One day at work he was served with divorce papers. Immediately he went home and asked for an explanation. His wife said: "For years I thought I was doing all I could to be a perfect wife for you. I was always here when you needed me. I fixed your meals. I patiently listened to you when you were excited about a new project. But you never shared *yourself* with me. You gave me your time but never your feelings. Never your support. Never your encouragement. I've tried and tried to reach you but never could I get through. I wish you could just be a regular person!"

The last thing Richard wanted was a divorce. So he asked his wife what he could do to help—the first time he ever asked her advice. She told him he would have to see a counselor if he wanted to save the marriage. So he reluctantly agreed.

Fortunately, the counselor was skilled enough to help Richard break through his defensive barriers. Richard realized that he had little to lose and much to gain by letting his wife and friends see his inner self. With the counselor's help Richard expressed some of the old feelings of fear and social inadequacy that had been buried for years. Richard learned that by allowing himself to be open and vulnerable, he was more likable than ever before. By trusting his wife and a few friends with regular expressions of his needs and hurts, he tore down the walls of defensiveness and was able to build new bridges of communication.

Now Richard says, "I only wish I had been brought to my new understanding of life years earlier."

How to Control Defensiveness

Feelings of defensiveness can be controlled. First, we need to have an acute awareness of the behaviors indicative of our feelings of resistance. Then we need to understand that God desires that we share ourselves with one another: "Bear one another's burdens, and thus fulfill the law of Christ" (Gal. 6:2). By dropping the barriers of defensiveness we will have a greater capacity to live in a more Christ-like manner. Following are some suggestions that will lead to the control of defensiveness.

Think Through the Goals of Your Relationships

In order to gain control of your defensiveness, it is helpful to ask: "Where am I going in my relationships? What am I trying to accomplish?" We know that defensive persons need to be in control. (In a sense we all have that need whether or not we are fully conscious of it.) They also have implied goals of privacy and superiority. But these goals do little to enhance the Christian's purpose of living in God's love. There is no sense of ministry with defensiveness.

Philippians 2:2 reads: "Make my joy complete by being of the same mind, maintaining the same love, united in spirit, intent on one purpose." This indicates that a major goal in relationships, particularly those of a Christian nature, is unity of spirit. A sense of cooperation, a need for give and take in one's communications, and a desire for fellowship is essential in any growing relationship; but the walls of defensiveness will usually work against a spirit of unity.

Remember Richard? Richard decided, after almost losing his marriage, that he had much to gain by being more attentive to his wife and acquaintances. Also, he decided that he no longer wanted the empty feeling that came with keeping all his emotions and reactions inside. The key to the change in Richard's heart was a willingness to examine the goals of his relationships. Rather than creating tension by his defensiveness, he tried to create an atmosphere of unity so a Christ-like love could be established within his relationships.

Be Willing to Confess Wrongs

Defensive people usually find it extremely difficult to say, "I was wrong." Or, if they do get around to admitting a fault, there usually is a "but" attached to the statement. For example, "I'll admit that I shouldn't have become so upset *but* what else can you expect when you are acting so rudely?" The atmosphere remains uneasy and unproductive.

It helps to be honest enough to specifically state one's areas of weakness. For example, an office worker who has a hard time accepting corrections from the boss, might say, "I know I overreact if anyone wants to point out a mistake to me, so I plan to concentrate on accepting feedback openly." Or, a spouse who tends to be overly critical might say, "I know my harshness frustrates you, and I'll work to cut it down." Open admissions of personal faults can go a long way toward creating an accommodating mood, can cause one to make specific plans to improve, and can put other people at ease.

Case Study

Ted and Nan seemed to be "experts" at keeping each other on the defensive. Nan was willing to make open confessions of her wrongs, but she usually sabotaged her openness by explaining to Ted how he was just as flawed as she, if not more so. When this happened Ted became defensive and withdrawn, which caused Nan to retreat into her own "emotional foxhole." After years of this merry-go-round, Nan realized that such defensiveness was only leading them downhill. So she approached Ted: "I'll concentrate on just getting my faults taken care of if you'll do the same with your faults. We will agree to weekly updates when we share how we are progressing." Ted was receptive to the idea. He realized that both would need to commit to a new kind of openness to enrich their marriage.

Allow for Other Points of View

Seeing issues in only black-and-white terms, usually assuming that we are right and other persons are wrong, easily leads to the point of drawing battle lines and engaging in war. Yet, realistically we know that not all issues can be neatly categorized as either right or wrong. Often, if two people have two separate feelings or impressions about a particular subject, both points of view may be valid.

Case Study

For example, Danny frequently heard the complaint from his wife that he was not very supportive of her needs. She shared with him her desire to have more intimate talks. She craved more of his emotional attention. But Danny, being quite defensive, ignored her pleas and stubbornly retorted, "You don't know how to appreciate the good things I do for you. You're just being selfish!" Of course, friction easily resulted.

In time and through counseling Danny realized that if his wife perceived him as being nonsupportive, he needed to acknowledge that she was entitled to her feelings. Though it was uncomfortable to hear such personal remarks, he cared enough about her feelings to try to understand why she felt as she did. He no longer responded defensively to remarks about his husbandly behavior. His tone was more accommodating: "I know that sometimes I'm not as sensitive as you would like me to be, but I'm working to show more support."

By allowing varying points of view, we acknowledge that persons have the right to their own feelings, impressions, and interpretations. What is important for one person may be trivial to another. What causes sharp emotional reactions from one person may be ignored by another. We must not simply assume that one person's perception is better or worse; people merely interpret their world differently. When allowance is made for this fact, defensiveness diminishes.

Seek to Put Others at Ease

Since defensiveness usually creates tensions and readily contributes to discord, a possible antidote would be to seek to be a harmonizer. We can look for opportunities to make others feel comfortable and seek to establish a reputation for being an encourager. Hebrews 10:24 states: "Let us consider how to stimulate one another to love and good deeds."

Betty recognized that she needed to be careful in her manner of communication. She genuinely desired to grow in her Christian faith, and she wanted to establish secure "comfort zones" in her relationships. She knew that by being an up-beat, encouraging person she would lessen her own tendency to feel defensive and at the same time she would help others feel at ease with her. So she began at home, by giving each family member at least one compliment per day. "Just like vitamins, we all have our minimum daily requirements of compliments." She also demonstrated genuine interest in the lives of her friends and neighbors. These actions lessened Betty's tendencies to close herself off from others.

God has made us for relationships. First, He desires us to have a personal relationship with Him through Jesus Christ. Second, He desires each of us to conduct our relations with others in such a way that they will see His love in our lives. As we love God our desire to love others increases; as we love others our ability to understand God increases. Such lives move closer to the fulfillment God has planned for them.

Questions for Further Thought

How do I exhibit defensive feelings? When am I obviously defensive? subtly defensive?

Why am I defensive? Do I have something to hide? Why am I afraid of what others might think of me?

What do I do that causes others to feel defensive? How can I establish a reputation as an encourager?

Where am I going in my relationships? Which feelings and behaviors indicate a forward progress?

How do my emotions reflect a positive self-esteem which means I able to feel good about myself in spite of my weaknesses?

How well do I understand God's unconditional love for me? How do I show that love in my relations with others?

3

Depression

Late one weekend night the phone beside my bed rang, waking me and my wife. Because of the odd hour I suspected it was my answering service giving me the message about someone in a crisis. Sure enough, I was told to call a woman, Donna, who was crying uncontrollably at her home. I had counseled Donna several months before. So I was curious about the nature of her emergency. When I reached Donna, she was crying desperately. She sobbed: "I've made so much progress over the past few months. I thought I'd never have to experience this low mood again. But now I feel as terrible as I've ever felt before. I hate being depressed. I just wish I could die!"

In my years of counseling I've met many men and women who, like Donna, have had one bout after another with depression. Year by year the number of people bothered by depression increases. In fact, in the past two decades our country has been experiencing an epidemic of depression. At any given point in time, as much as 15 percent of the population experiences feelings of depression. That means that today over 30 million people will feel depressed, half of whom may be labeled as seriously or severely depressed. And while most of us may not have extended battles with depression, virtually no one is completely immune from it. We have imperfect personalities which interact with an imperfect sinful world, and therefore we will have experiences with this emotion in some form or fashion.

Depression *is a feeling of sadness and dejection accompanied by a gloomy mind-set. Depression usually involves a sense of mental dullness that manifests itself in a variety of symptoms including poor concentration and pessimistic thinking patterns. It can last anywhere from a few hours to several months or, in rare cases, even years. Depression is distinguished from simple unhappiness by being more prolonged than circumstances reasonably warrant.*

Use the following checklist of symptoms that often accompany depression to assess your vulnerability to it. The more symptoms you can identify with, the more likely you are to have bouts with depression.

1 Easily fatigued; evident loss of energy
2 Feeling of hopelessness
3 Inability to enjoy normally pleasant events
4 Altered eating habits: either overeating or loss of appetite
5 Slowed sexual drive
6 Indifference toward family and friends
7 Feeling of ineptitude toward tasks
8 Change in sleep habits: insomnia, waking early, sleeping too much, etc.
9 Desire to die
10 More pronounced physical aches and pains
11 Disregard for order in one's life, manifested by drug or alcohol abuse, promiscuity, etc.
12 Irritability and holding grudges
13 Poor motivation to start projects
14 Inconsistent mental concentration
15 Tendency to be overly critical
16 Seemingly diminished physical strength
17 Sense of judgment negatively altered
18 Crying easily
19 Tendency to fantasize
20 Frequent self put-downs
21 Feeling that life is worthless
22 Prominent distrust
23 Easily worried
24 Dwelling on the past
25 Poor work habits
26 Frequent bouts with feelings of guilt and low personal value.

This list of depression characteristics indicates that the emotion varies widely among individuals. It is obvious that when a person is depressed, life readily loses its vigor and vitality. We will definitely want to minimize depression as much as possible since it is a major detractor from the life of pleasure that God wishes us to have.

Causes of Depression

I strongly believe that a thorough understanding of a problem emotion can be the crucial first step in overcoming it. So we are brought to the question: What causes depression? What are some major underlying problems rooted in this emotion?

Negative-Thinking Patterns

A depressed person has a pronounced tendency to think about matters from a negative perspective. For example, when a person becomes depressed, it is much easier to decide what is wrong about a relationship rather than what is right. Or a depressed person does not focus on what good can come from a task but rather speaks pointedly about why the task is tedious or boring. When an individual allows negative thinking to run rampant, depression easily arises. In fact, negative thinking is both a root cause of depression and a perpetuator of the problem.

It is important to note that though a person is currently caught in a negative-thinking pattern, he may not always have had such tendencies. Many times I've heard people say: "I haven't always been this way. I used to be much more optimistic about things." But whether the negative thinking is only temporary or is a deeply ingrained habit, it is like poison to one's emotions. People should not become unrealistic to the point of dwelling only on "sugar sweet" thoughts. A balance is needed in the way an individual thinks matters through. We are told in Proverbs 23:7 "As he thinks within himself, so is he."

Case Study

Jeff was entrenched in one of the most difficult periods in his adult life. His business was on shaky grounds due to the prevailing state of the economy. His children's interests had grown outside the home. His wife seemed engrossed in her own activities and didn't give him the attention he felt he deserved. Jeff became absorbed by what he didn't like in his life, and his feelings of discouragement got so completely out of hand that he fell into a full pattern of chronic depression. He didn't exert much mental effort toward constructive problem solving in his business. Rather, he kept ruminating over past mistakes and pessimistic forecasts. When he considered his family circumstances he became cynical. "After all I've done for them, I get no appreciation." He was much different from his normal cheerful self. He regularly lapsed into times when he would dwell solely on the flaws of each family member. His criticisms weren't completely wrong, but they were given too much prominence. Jeff's negative thinking style caused normal discouragement to blossom into a full pattern of depression.

When Jeff came to my counseling office, we quickly focused on his prevailing negativism. He became aware that he had become his own worst enemy by calling attention to all that was wrong. In essence, he had made the mistake of viewing his world as being either all black or all white. As Jeff was challenged to seek out the things that were positive in his life, he found a new attitude. He learned that he could exert a positive influence on people by finding good things to comment on. While his problems didn't necessarily go away overnight, Jeff learned that he didn't have to completely cave in to them.

Unresolved Anger

I have never met a person who suffered from depression who did not have some underlying anger. That's a pretty strong statement, yet it's true. Depression virtually always has repressed anger at its base.

When we think of anger, we often have a mental picture of a person prone to hostile outbursts, and hurling insults. While anger is often portrayed in this open, obnoxious style, it is not limited to these manifestations. In fact, more often than not, anger is handled in more subtle, "beneath the surface" ways: inner feelings of resentment, critical attitudes, chronic pessimism, tension, frustration, and irritability. Anger is a diverse emotion that causes depression when it is clung to for inappropriate lengths of time.

Almost all depressed people have difficulty in knowing how to bring their anger to completion. Many individuals have habits of openly expressing anger in destructive rather than constructive ways, or have developed the tendency of repressing anger to the extent that a sour inner attitude develops. In either case the unresolved anger lingers inside the individual's subconscious mind and is like a mold which takes root and grows in damp darkness.

Case Study

Rhonda, now in her early thirties, had always enjoyed relationships to their fullest. She was attractive, energetic, and had all the traits that made her look successful. Yet she was aware that her fun-loving nature may have worked against her because she never learned how to adequately handle the stresses of confrontation.

When Rhonda married, she had the notion that she and her husband, a budding, young surgeon, would have a life of sheer delight. She never expected that arguments and anger would be a part of her marriage. Imagine her reaction when she first realized that her husband wasn't all she expected. She was sorely disappointed. Rhonda developed a habit early in her marriage of repressing her negative feelings. She was afraid she would say the wrong things. She didn't know how to express her frustrations without being offensive. When her friends and social acquaintances began displaying annoying weaknesses she would merely hold her feelings inside herself.

As the years went by, Rhonda's habit of "stuffing" her negative feelings continued. Her fun-loving nature began to gradually diminish as her inner feelings of frustration grew. A sense of negativism developed inwardly and it was not long before she began showing some of the classic symptoms of depression. Her outlook on life became critical. She felt poorly about herself as a wife and friend, though she couldn't exactly say why. She began to retreat from the sort of indepth interchanges that she once had thrived on. Rhonda had repressed her anger so long that it became an emotional cancer. She became a victim of her failure to openly resolve her aggravations.

To reverse this pattern, Rhonda had to learn that there were times when it was actually helpful to share her irritated feelings. She came to understand that she was stunting her own emotional growth by choosing to keep her feelings trapped tightly inside herself. By expressing her feelings carefully and responsibly she was able to rid herself of these repressed emotions.

Difficulty Handling Rejection

In a large percentage of cases, depression is due to problem relationships. Since we have been created to love and to be loved, it is only natural that we will have an extra measure of expectation and sensitivity when we become close to someone else. Because of this inborn desire and vulnerability within close relationships, we can become depressed if we experience serious or repeated rejections.

Case Study

Patrick grew up with a strong feeling of being rejected by his father. While he worked incessantly to please his dad, Patrick consistently felt that he could never "make the grade." He remembers that his father specifically told him that he would never amount to anything. As an adult Patrick carried over these uneasy feelings into his other relationships. In his work as an architect he was often so tentative that his work was frequently turned down by his superiors. This served to reinforce his sense of feeling unworthy. At home he was never certain if his wife truly meant it when she said, "I love you." In his mind, he could focus only on the times when she had complained to him or criticized him. Patrick's background of being shunned by his father made it hard for him to see himself as being lovable and competent.

In therapy Patrick's major task was to recognize that the rejection he had received from his father was not merited; rather, it was more of a commentary on his father's need to be superior. Patrick was merely the victim of his father's own inner inadequacies. By learning to come to grips mentally with the reasons for his past struggles, Patrick was able to get out of the habit of assuming that all other significant people would treat him just as his father did.

As a person satisfactorily gives and receives love in a rewarding way (without ulterior motives), life gains purpose. Contentment occurs. Look for and expect successful ties to be made with others. Yet, because we have fallen from the perfection originally given to mankind by God, flaws will eventually show up in any relationship. This means that while it is natural to seek satisfaction with others, it is also natural to receive disappointments and rejections. A person who does not adequately acknowledge this fact is making himself a prime candidate for repeated experiences with depression.

Wrong Priorities

God has a way of being direct when He tells us what it takes to have a life of fulfillment. For example, He tells us to love Him with our entire being (Matt. 22:37); He encourages us to share His love with those with whom we come in contact (1 John 4:11); to give priority to our family lives (1 Tim. 5:8); to give priority to a Bible-believing, New Testament church (1 Tim. 3:15). God has outlined a plan for our lives that, if faithfully followed, can bring us the joy we all desire.

Individuals—particularly Christians—who fall into a period of depression, usually admit they have gone counter to the priorities God has given us in the Bible. I have often talked with depressed Christians who admit that they have not done all they know to do in following God's will for their lives. For example, a depressed businessman may admit that he has placed his career desires ahead of his spiritual or family needs. Or, perhaps a person knows of the Scripture's instruction regarding a temperate, kind nature, but has given in to tendencies of extreme competitiveness. A depressed woman may have allowed a finicky nature to displace her usually gentle spirit. Even though depressed people know what is biblically right, in spite of their knowledge, they often blindly pursue other matters.

Case Study

Deborah had a tendency to knowingly pursue behaviors that were clearly inappropriate. She could quote all sorts of Scripture references about patience, love, and kindness. Yet in her family life she was often volatile in her communications. In fact, she would state very honestly: "I know I'm wrong to be so insistent with my family, but I just can't help it." As we explored the reasons for her emotional explosiveness, we discovered that her lifestyle gave first priority to her demands. All other demands were secondary, so she was stuck in a rut of depression and tension.

I challenged her to recognize that she could choose the ways she would conduct herself. She could follow Deborah's "rules" of living and continue experiencing her current frustration, or she could choose to follow God's ways and experience the peace that comes from that lifestyle. By recognizing that she was responsible for selecting the priorities in her life, Deborah became increasingly aware that her emotions were contingent on her choices.

If we view depression as being caused in part by inappropriate priorities, then we may presume that God allows depression so that we will recognize our need to put our lives in proper order.

Feelings of Incompetence

A depressed person also struggles with self-degradation. Deep down, he has endorsed the thought: "I don't have what it takes to get through trying situations." The self put-down is evident.

Actually, no human being has the complete ability to solve all of life's problems in his own strength. However, we have a God who is willing to supply us with the ability we need to endure hardships. Consequently, when an individual gets caught in a rut of depression, he fails to use the capability that God so willingly offers.

Case Study

Mary Lynn came to my counseling office because she had recurring problems with depression. We discussed her opinion of herself. Predictably, she said that she had rarely felt she had much to offer others. Whether she focused on her personality traits, intelligence, or ability to perform routine tasks, she would label herself "incompetent." No wonder she had problems with persistent low moods.

One day Mary Lynn told me how a friend had shared with her the Scripture verse: "For God has not given us a spirit of timidity, but of power and love and discipline" (1 Tim. 1:7). Her eyes sparkled with excitement as she said, "Les, if this verse applies to me that means I'm not so incompetent after all!" With that insight she began thinking differently about herself. She knew that the God who had created her was willing to empower her with all the tools she needed to face life.

Biological Problems

I should point out that while depression is most often perpetuated by intrapersonal struggles, there are times when biochemical difficulties add to the problem. In one's body are neurotransmitters (such as serotonin and norepinephrine) that help regulate emotional and mental stability. If these transmitters are out of balance, the brain may not be able to properly maintain stability. When this happens the depression is said to be biochemical.

Also, there are some medications given for other physical problems (high blood pressure, for example) that may cause depression. Consumption of alcohol or illicit drugs can increase an individual's tendency toward low moods. In light of these physical possibilities, it is wise for a person who has significantly deep and lasting struggles with depression to be thoroughly examined by a competent physician or psychiatrist.

Case Study

Now in his early fifties, Sam had lived a lifetime trying to please anyone who came into his path. Seemingly he had been the ideal father and husband. He was loyal to his company, and he was active in both civic and church affairs. But though Sam's life might have looked good to an outsider, inwardly he felt no joy because he knew he had lived as a nice guy for all the wrong reasons. He was chronically depressed.

Sam admitted that he had always done what was right because he lived in constant fear of being rejected. "I was always afraid that my boys would be ashamed of me, or that my wife would turn her interests to someone else. I did all the right things, but I never could feel happy about it because I just knew something bad would happen." He was super-sensitive to any criticism or hint of rejection. It was easy for him to develop a deeply ingrained sense of pessimism. He was constantly looking for things to go wrong.

Through the years Sam developed a very critical way of thinking about others and about himself. He would nurse grudges and harbor resentments because he felt that people didn't really seem to understand him or care about his needs. (He didn't realize that he "encouraged" others to misunderstand him because he played the Mr. Nice Guy role.) He often felt anger and frustration but rarely expressed them in an open manner. He viewed himself as a person who was an emotional wreck, which lowered his feelings of self-esteem. Because he harbored distasteful feelings inside, he could easily convince himself that he had low worth and value.

When Sam came to my counseling office, depression was firmly established as a way of life for him. He felt hopeless about his future because his past had been so unpleasant. He wanted to change, but had no confidence he could rearrange his lifelong habits. So we approached his problems with a "positive stubbornness." That is, we set our minds tenaciously on a goal of contentment for Sam and aimed for success, knowing there would be some trials and pitfalls along the way.

Sam liked the idea of proceeding with positive stubbornness. He had rarely had a sense of tenacity toward anything. The first thing we worked to change was Sam's beliefs and opinions about himself. If Sam could believe that he was valuable before God, efforts to alleviate his emotional difficulties would be easier. As Sam's level of self-esteem grew, he became more strongly motivated to discover why he responded so negatively to trying circumstances.

Sam still had periodic low moods. Being imperfect, he didn't change himself overnight. By rearranging his thoughts about himself and by analyzing the reasons behind his moods he exercised fairly consistent control over his depression.

How to Control Depression

Depression is not an easy emotion to conquer. In fact, it is quite normal for even healthy, mature Christians to experience it on occasions. So we need not live with the illusion that this sour feeling can be eradicated forever. However, depression does not have to dominate our lives. By following these principles, we can minimize or alleviate our bouts with depression.

Examine Your Foundation for Self-Confidence

Ten years ago a land developer purchased a huge tract of land on the outskirts of a big city with the idea of creating a fantastic residential area. Seemingly overnight his tractors and earth-movers swept through the hilly terrain to make way for the meandering boulevards that would lead to luxurious estates. As the developer's scheme unfolded, it was heralded as being the ultimate in suburban living. Treelined streets and elegant homes indeed made this a luxurious neighborhood.

But that was ten years ago. Now if you would take a drive through the same area you would notice bumps and potholes in the roads. "For Sale" signs are prominent on an inordinately large number of lawns. Why? What happened to this fantasy land? The developer created his plans and built his homes without making allowances for the peculiar kind of soil found there. The soil was very elastic and prone to frequent shifts. It provided a poor foundation for both roads and houses. Bricks crumbled and fell off outside walls. Roads buckled and cracked. The developer's dream turned into a homeowner's nightmare.

In a sense, many people live psychologically with the same kind of problem. They have grand schemes but little in-depth planning for emotional stability. Too often these people depend on the approval of others or for personal achievements to give them their ultimate sense of strength and security.

Case Study

Ray thrived on the fact that he was considered the very best in his profession and he was constantly pampered by a family who doted on him and catered to his every whim. But, when his practice took a downward spiral and his family began turning away from his ego needs, he plummeted to the very depths of depression. His foundation for happiness was not sturdy enough to carry him through difficult situations.

In therapy, Ray learned that he was trying to build his sense of emotional stability on a foundation of performances and "approval ratings." While he knew that he had a loving family and that he was good in his profession, he learned that the only true foundation for personal stability was to be found in his relationship with God.

First Peter 5:6–7 tells us: "Humble yourselves, therefore, under the mighty hand of God, that He may exalt you at the proper time, casting all your anxiety upon Him, because He cares for you." God is the anchor that steadies us in times of trouble. He is the foundation on which confidence and stability are built. By committing our lives to Him and looking to His word for strength and guidance, we can have the assurance that He will properly carry us in our time of need.

Pinpoint the times when depression is most likely to occur. A family member is consistently rebellious. Your job is no longer satisfying. Friends are not there when you need them the most. Your money runs out. When these circumstances cause a person to be seriously depressed, that is an indication such a person has looked to human, earthly things for personal stability. (It is normal to be somewhat discouraged with personal misfortune. I am referring here to inappropriate depression.)

Isaiah 28:16 says: "Behold, I am laying in Zion a stone, a tested stone, a costly cornerstone for the foundation, firmly placed. He who believes in it will not be disturbed." That cornerstone is Jesus Christ. Placing Him in control of our emotions, we are able to master depression. When Christ controls our lives, we are willing to submit to His teachings and study His word to receive guidance for our attitudes, emotions, and behaviors.

Keep Lines of Communication Open

Depressed people tend to have many old feelings repressed. Such squelched anxiety, anger, or guilt can fester in one's subconscious mind to the extent that depression results. To counter this problem, find someone with whom you can share these inner feelings. There is a lot of truth in the old axiom: "Confession is good for the soul."

Ecclesiastes 4:9–10 states: "Two are better than one because they have a good return for their labor. For if either of them falls, the one will lift up his companion." God has given us human relations as a gift to experience the joy of loving fellowship. There is no better time to share with friends in an open manner than when depression begins.

To do so requires a certain amount of unfamiliar boldness because most of us are shy about revealing our deep feelings. Knowing that it can be helpful to clear the air with honest statements about one's feelings, an individual could ask himself: "How beneficial is it for me to harbor hidden resentments?" Usually, when a person realizes the detrimental effects of holding back, he can be spurred to take a deep breath and express his thoughts and needs in a firm but gentle way.

Develop a Giving Heart

Usually a depressed person has become caught in the rut of a self-centered thought pattern. The focus is on *me:* my hurts, my situation. And while it is helpful to openly express those feelings and to gently confront the people who contribute to an unhappy situation, it is best to keep a balance in one's communications by remembering that other people also have needs. In fact, shifting one's mental energies onto someone else's needs can bring healing to both parties.

Case Study

Nick, was depressed because his wife had unexpectedly filed a petition for divorce. For weeks, Nick was so distraught that his marital problems completely dominated all his conversations. Fortunately, a friend noticed this exaggerated tendency and made Nick aware of it. He suggested: "Nick, try to go through conversations focusing on someone else's feelings. It could help you." Nick tried it, and as he became more attuned to other people's needs, he was able to place his own emotional problems in better perspective.

My suggestion to the depressed person at first glance could seem insensitive, but it is not: Don't take yourself so seriously. It is so easy to become wrapped up in your own problems. You are not the center of the universe. Remind yourself that people in the world around you have problems, too. A balanced focus on both your needs and the needs of others is necessary and appropriate.

Focus Daily on God's Concern for You

When depression comes to a person, God can seem to be thousands of miles away. In fact, some depressed people entertain the notion that God doesn't exist at all. But regardless of what we think, God's love is always available. The problem is not that He has withdrawn from us; the problem is that we draw away from Him.

Depressed persons often ask, "If God loves me so much, why doesn't He do a better job in demonstrating it?" The answer is easy enough to give, but it requires both faith and action on the human's part to receive it. You see, Ephesians 2:4–5 explains that God has demonstrated His love to us in sending His Son, Jesus Christ, to take the punishment for our sins by dying on a criminal's cross. "But God, being rich in mercy, because of IIis great love with which He loved us, even when we were dead in our transgressions, made us alive together with Christ (by grace you have been saved)." But this love did not end 2000 years ago with Jesus' death on the cross; it is the same today as it was then. Furthermore, God has given us in Scripture a plan for joyful living. By examining God's Word, it is possible for the depressed person to recognize God's care for His own.

A major reason we have difficulty comprehending God's concern is that we tend to humanize Him, assuming His love will be as inconsistent as a friend's, parent's, or spouse's love. However, remember that God is without sin, is unwavering in His traits, and therefore is perfectly consistent in His care for us. So as a person places his faith in the truth of God's unchanging love, depression decreases, and a sense of optimism and self-value develops. The person who accepts God's love also accepts the self-worth that follows it.

Develop a Plan of Action

Depression is a problem that occurs repeatedly if the individual does not make deliberate efforts to stay on top of it. Consequently, a plan for daily action is in order.

When a depressed person gets to the point where he is ready for a daily action plan, I encourage him to consider his needs in four separate categories: spiritual, physical, emotional, human relationships. Specific plans for use in each of these areas can be spelled out and regularly followed.

Case Study

Shannon came to my counseling office seeking help for her depression. We spent several sessions exploring her background and thinking patterns so she might understand the reasons for her emotional struggles. As her insights deepened, it became apparent to both Shannon and me that she was ready to make some changes in her lifestyle, and we decided on the following action plan.

1. Shannon knew she had strayed from the Lord, so she decided to join a women's weekly Bible study in a local church. In addition, she decided that she would spend at least thirty minutes each day in personal devotion time.

2. Since being depressed, Shannon had become lazy about her household and physical needs. She made a schedule for doing a certain amount of chores each day, thereby not letting her work pile up. Also, she would take a one- or two-mile walk three or four evenings a week with her daughter.

3. Shannon knew she should develop positive traits that would lead to a healthy emotional nature, and she chose to exhibit the fruit of the Spirit listed in Galatians 5:22–23. Each day she made one of those traits—for example, gentleness—a goal for the day by keeping it prominent in her thoughts and actions.

4. Finally, in her efforts to bring deeper satisfaction to her relationships, Shannon determined to initiate at least one meaningful conversation a day with each member of her family, communicating her concern for their needs and expressing her own needs rather than repressing them.

As Shannon discovered, it is possible to chart a course of action that can draw oneself closer to the plan that God has for each of us. As we acknowledge the fact that God wants us to know contentment, we can become partners with Him in the effort to bring depression under control.

Questions for Further Thought

How fully do I acknowledge God's love for me? Is this just intellectual knowledge, or have I truly integrated His love into my style of thinking?

How do I hold resentments and grudges? Which problems need to be openly and lovingly confronted? Am I willing to forgive when others do wrong? Am I willing to forgive myself?

Do I tend to be tuned in too exclusively to my hurts and needs? Am I willing to turn my attention to the needs and feelings of other people?

Am I willing to commit to an action plan or am I waiting for someone else to take the initiative to get me out of my depression?

What kind of action plan can I devise to keep my depression under control?

4

Envy

Bryan was exasperated. "I don't know why I have such a hard time liking Jim. He seems to be a nice guy, and I'm not particularly angry with him about anything. But it just seems that he gets all the lucky breaks. Even though we joined the company at about the same time, he got promoted faster than I did. And when we're together in a group of people, everyone seems to be attracted to him. But for some reason, he just turns me off. I can't really explain why."

I knew exactly what Bryan's problem was. He was envious of Jim. Bryan was a bright fellow with a good future in his chosen profession. But here he was being shown up by this "wonder-boy." Jim's success was too much for Bryan to handle. Jim was receiving the attention that Bryan wanted for himself. Bryan didn't acknowledge it, yet his subtle anger was evident.

We all have known feelings of envy at one time or another. Our highly-competitive culture teaches us (either subtly or openly) to be wary of the one who has what we want. We seem to have a hard time just enjoying the fact that someone else can experience gains and rewards.

Envy *is a subtle form of anger gone awry, and can be defined as a feeling of resentment or discontent about the advantages, possessions, or successes of another. Resentment stems from the fact that another person has attained something which one wishes to attain for oneself. That is, there is a grudge feeling because someone else has what I think I deserve. Envy is different from mere wants and desires because it involves bitterness and malicious thoughts.*

Manifestations of Envy

Examples of envy are plentiful in our lives. A husband envies his wife who easily makes friends, while he has to work to keep a conversation going. A woman in a Bible study session envies another's knowledge of deep scriptural truths. An unhappy wife envies a friend whose husband is warm and receptive. A middle-class couple envies another couple who has inherited a large sum of money. Single persons envy the married, and vice versa. And on and on.

Envious persons tend to have one or more of the following characteristics. Perhaps you can identify with some traits. Envious people:

1 Work extremely hard to present themselves right and good.
2 Find it easy to examine others with a critical eye.
3 Have hidden feelings of inferiority.
4 Readily complain about not getting fair treatment or good breaks.
5 Have an insatiable desire for success.
6 Need much overt recognition of their achievements.
7 Enjoy the feeling of being in control.
8 Tend to be status-conscious.
9 Are impressed by titles.
10 Cringe at the idea of examining their own weaknesses.
11 Find it hard to pay compliments.
12 Have difficulty giving generously.
13 Tend to hold grudges.
14 Keep score of their own good deeds and of the good deeds of others.
15 Prefer to avoid successful people.
16 Are willing to pass along negative rumors about a successful person.
17 Often put on a false front in order to appear impressive.
18 Have frequent fantasies of what it would be like at the top.
19 Base their self-image on their performance.
20 Prone to hold "pet peeves."

Envy is a broad-based emotion that ruins one's emotional nature. It can strike at virtually any time or setting. First Peter 2:1–2 advises: "Putting aside all malice and all guile and hyprocrisy and envy and all slander, like newborn babes, long for the pure milk of the word." Since envy can divert a person's attention from God's Word, we are directed to set it aside. Envy's capacity for destruction is too strong to be left unrestrained.

Causes of Envy

As with virtually all emotions the use of envy is determined by certain key inner factors. A person's use of envy indicates that there are underlying issues that need to be explored and resolved. Following are some of the reasons that a person can have struggles with envy.

Heavy Emphasis on Personal Rights

During the past couple decades, our society has seen one battle after another for the individual's rights: civil rights, worker's rights, women's rights, children's rights, teacher's rights, and so on. It is not wrong to seek to implant a sense of fairness in social issues. But when the emphasis on personal rights is blown so far out of proportion, it creates emotional problems. Our society has come to a point where individuals can be unhealthily obsessed with getting their just rewards. A demanding nature and an over-ambitious sense of expectations can result.

Case Study

Gail frequently struggled with feelings of envy because a co-worker obviously enjoyed a favored-status position with her boss. This co-worker was the daughter of the boss's best friend. So often they had lunch together or had a friendly chat in the hall. Gail watched them closely and when she felt her cohort was given special treatment in any way, she would complain to herself: "Hey, what about my rights? I've worked here longer and I work harder than she does." Certainly Gail was not entirely wrong in her assertions. Yet there was a danger that she could become so wrapped up in her desires to have her rights met that her productivity would falter significantly. Gail needed to learn to exercise a delicate balance between standing up for her rights while maintaining a proper regard of her responsibilities.

Certainly we need a positive sense of self-preservation in interpersonal matters, but I also encourage people to place greater emphasis on their own responsibilities in a given situation. That is, rather than asking "What are my rights?" I encourage people to ponder the question "What are my responsibilities?" With this shift in mental focus, the individual is less prone to envy.

Taking Other's Successes Too Personally

Envy involves a close feeling of identification or empathy toward the person being envied. For example, I have never envied a highly skilled seamstress because I never developed a desire to sew. However, I can easily become envious of a person with tremendous social skills because I have a great desire to be a "people person." Obviously, envy first assumes a feeling of being in the other person's shoes.

While it is natural to have feelings of identification with other people of like interests and desires, problems occur when we carry this too far. It is possible for an individual to become too emotionally connected to the actions of another to the extent that envy erupts. It is possible to experience hurt and bitterness because of excessively close identification with another person. Estrangement and alienation result because an undesired difference becomes highlighted, an indication that the projection is too strong.

Case Study

Betty could hardly bear to be in her sister's company. June had a fine Christian husband, a happy home, and three model children. They were respected in their church and community. Betty, however, had experienced a divorce and was forced to work extremely hard to support herself and her young daughter. She lacked all the wonderful family happiness that June had. Consequently, Betty shunned June and thought of her with sarcastic overtones. While Betty knew and accepted many other women who experienced marital satisfaction, she couldn't handle her sister's blessings. Betty's close identification with her sister was the major factor in her envy. Clearly, Betty's greatest need was to develop some emotional detachment from her sister so she could replace her subjective responses with objective thinking.

Desire for Selfish Gain

Envy always is precipitated by desire or yearning. We all want things we don't have: material things such as money, a fine home, or nice clothes; or abstract matters such as happiness, good communications, or emotional composure. As long as these wants are held in a realistic perspective they will cause no particular harm.

When a person has a long, unrealistic wish list and is in constant search for some ideal object or experience that will insure personal pleasure, it is usually an indication that he needs an ego boost. Such a person is prone to coveting and all the emotional turmoil that accompanies it.

The individual who is overanxious about personal gain is motivated by the fear of being shown up. That is the ulterior motive behind his wish to become superior over others. In this sense, envy involves a desire to build up self, even if it is at someone else's expense. One's mental focus is on me, my aspirations, my wants. This can explain why some successful businessmen will become workaholics, pushing themselves far beyond the normal boundaries. Having a need to top others causes people to always strive to gain just a little more, and finally more is never enough. Besides, there is always someone else who seems to have still more.

Overemphasis on Status and Achievement

Envious people have mulled over the idea of success and status and developed strong opinions about "the good life." Be it family living, financial matters, or religious activities, envious people have a firm notion about what it takes to be tops in that area. A competitive spirit is prominent.

In my counseling practice I have found that envy can be experienced by people at any level of socioeconomic status, intellectual functioning, or religious persuasion. This emotion is so widespread because most people grow up under heavy scrutiny of their external performances. Teenage boys learn quickly to judge themselves on athletic ability or social prowess. Girls are evaluated according to physical beauty or personality. The need to prove themselves by their performance continues into adulthood. Churches, too, encourage all their members to outwardly demonstrate their God-given gifts. Most of us feel as if we are living in a fishbowl with people staring at us, waiting to judge the next performance.

Consequently, we crave recognition in the positive aspects of our lives. When we notice that someone else is achieving the status and recognition that we desire for ourselves, we selfishly yearn for the same. There is in all this an unspoken notion that we cannot accept ourselves for who or what we are. We want to be something higher, more appealing. We can be so programmed to reach further or to climb higher that we feel slighted when we are surpassed by someone who has "arrived."

Case Study

Kyle grew up in a home where he learned that superperformance was the way to get the love and affection that was so important to him. Being the third child of four he felt that he had to work extra hard for recognition because the older two brothers had already proven their skills in many areas while his younger sister seemed to get all the attention she wanted by just looking cute. So Kyle turned to the two things he knew he could do well, sports and academics. He pushed hard to excel in both basketball and baseball. And he did all he could to make high grades. He assumed that if he gained some status in these areas, he would receive the desired pats on the back.

But Kyle learned a disillusioning lesson. He often found that even when he stretched himself to his upper limits, he met someone else who was a little better. And what was worse, that someone was often one of his brothers. When Kyle scored the most points in a high school basketball game, his coach pulled him aside and said: "I can remember four years ago your brother was the high scorer against the same team." This infuriated Kyle. Whether it was at home, school, or church, Kyle felt as if his achievements would be compared to someone else who had also done well. At times he felt like giving up his quest for high status, but if he didn't perform he would get *no* recognition. Envy was a close companion to Kyle because he was so concerned with achievements.

Kyle was consumed by a competitive nature and was unable to feel satisfied with his own successes. He needed to learn that success in life did not come from being superior to others. Kyle needed to recognize that his self-worth was a by-product of God's love for him and his personal value would not go up or down depending on superiority or inferiority of performance.

Inability to Share

Inherent in envy is difficulty in sharing the happiness and joys of other people. The envious person tends to be so consumed with what he wishes to have that another person's good fortune serves only to remind him that he doesn't have those things (or status). The focus is on my wants, not another's pleasure.

One woman remained unmarried while many of her friends were meeting their knights in shining armor and taking their turns at the wedding altar. At first, she seemed to take her friends' good fortune in stride, but her envious feelings began to surface when friend after friend had a baby. She had strong maternal feelings and felt cheated when others experienced the thrill that she could only dream of. Her reaction was to cut herself off from her old friends because she was not able to share in their happiness.

Sharing is an art form. This is particularly true when a person has the chance to share in the happy moments of another. Such sharing involves the ability to set aside one's personal preferences and wishes in order to become absorbed in the good fortune of some else. When a person shares another's personal victories, critical thinking and personal strivings are set aside in favor of empathy and a giving spirit—a complete contradiction to the nature of envy.

Case Study

Greg struggled with an inordinate amount of pent-up rage. Outwardly, he was the picture of composure. He had a smooth voice and a pleasant smile. But hardly a day passed without Greg feeling some sort of resentment or bitterness toward a co-worker or family member. Greg's real problem was envy.

Greg's life could be described in one word: average. He was not particularly handsome, but he wasn't ugly either. He had his share of friends, but was never the center of attention. His grades had been adequate, not high. Greg moved through his early life somewhat unnoticed.

For many years Greg was hardly aware of his average status. That is, he basically felt O.K. about himself, sensing no particular need to make any major adjustment in his behaviors. He married an average woman while he was in college, and began his career as a computer salesman—things any normal young man was expected to do.

A few years later, Greg's job required him to travel. Suddenly, he was exposed to a wide variety of materialistic people and circumstances. He enjoyed all the excitement and stimulation found at popular night spots. He had opportunities to rub shoulders with the "in crowd," a very, fun-seeking lifestyle. And he liked it. He saw this lifestyle as a step up.

When Greg returned home from these trips he would frequently think about the people who had so many of the things he never had enjoyed in his humdrum lifestyle. He would daydream: "I wish I could be free like that. Boy, wouldn't it be neat to be able to drive a sports car and come and go whenever I want. Those people have it made!"

But reality would bring Greg down to earth. His envy grew as he realized that the swinging night life was not available to him because he had a wife and three kids to support. As time wore on, Greg's problem with this envy worsened. He would closely watch how other people would buy things just for the fun of it; things like boats, or exotic vacations, or flashy clothes. He allowed envy to take him to the point of disillusionment with himself and his lifestyle.

Greg's turnaround came during one of the low points in his life. His only daughter, six years old, whom he loved dearly, became severely ill, to the point of near-death. Six days of her two-week hospital stay were spent in the intensive care unit. The whole family was in need of emotional support and prayer. When his daughter began to improve, Greg realized that during his time of intense need not one of his "swinging" acquaintances visited him or offered encouragement by phone. Not one! No doubt they had heard of his daughter's illness through various contacts, but apparently they were so caught up in living life in their own hedonistic way that his troubles meant nothing to them.

Because of this experience Greg made a new promise to himself. He determined that he would not look to other people to determine what he should have in order to experience the "good life." He recognized that the things of this world are often too superficial and only temporarily satisfying. Rather than envying others for what they had, he was determined to be satisfied with the things in his life that really mattered. With this mindset he launched into an effort to discover God's will for him and his purpose in life as a father and husband.

How to Control Envy

Envy has no useful place in the person who is seeking to live in God's will. Galatians 5:26 states: "Let us not become boastful, challenging one another, envying one another." Envy is a detraction from living the

Spirit-filled life offered to us by God. These suggestions can help to gain control over envy.

Accept Yourself As You Are

Envious people lack contentment with their current position in life, seeking something that will make them seem more adequate than they believe themselves to be. Acceptance of oneself is measured by performance or acquisitions.

Someone once said to me: "I think I could accept myself if I had a few positive things going for me. But how can I accept myself when I don't like the way I'm living?" My response was to refer to Romans 5:8: "But God demonstrates His own love toward us, in that while we were yet sinners, Christ died for us." In other words, you can accept yourself because God took you where you were and gave you sufficiency in everything through Christ. If God loves you enough to save you and use you right where you are, then you do have value. That means you no longer have to worry about what you should do or how you should look to become acceptable. You'll feel a great relief from social pressures because the intensity of one's envy is in opposite proportion to the level of one's self-acceptance.

Keep Earthly Gains in Perspective

The greatest treasure we can have is the Spirit of Jesus Christ dwelling within us. First Timothy 6:6–7 reads: "But godliness actually is a means of great gain, when accompanied by contentment. For we have brought nothing into the world, so we cannot take anything out of it either." While we can be easily brainwashed into believing that such things as material wealth, popularity, and social suaveness are the ultimate in life, remember that contentment in Christ offers more.

The person who seeks to gain mental control of envy will have to address the question of priorities. An envious person is usually one who places *tangible* gains (money, acclaim, personal appearance) at the top of the list of priorities. While some of these things are necessary and harmless in moderation, Jesus, in Matthew 6:33 says: "But seek first His kingdom and His righteousness; and all these things shall be added to you." We are further promised that as we seek after the desires of God, He will ably supply all we need: "My God shall supply all your needs according to His riches in glory in Christ Jesus" (Phil. 4:9).

Set Your Own Goals Based on Your Convictions

Although envy can be controlled as a person begins to seriously examine his top priorities, it is important to set goals based on personal conviction and to stay away from the trap of establishing objectives merely to compete with others. That leads to problems. When one pursues priorities merely to prove himself, envy sneaks into the picture.

Case Study

When Bruce was a college student, he made the decision to give himself to God because he felt a strong need to get his life in proper perspective. But years later he realized he had allowed himself to set spiritual goals based on what he saw other Christians doing. For instance, as Bruce saw other people give time and money to the church, he would do the same because he didn't want to be shown up. He was attending Bible studies not so much for personal discipleship, but because he wanted to look good to his friends. Bruce decided that he needed to completely rethink his personal goals without fear of measuring up to other Christians. He found his motivation, instead, in his genuine desire to please God.

A person who lives with envy is constantly "looking over his shoulder" to see where others are in comparison to his position. Life is lived in fear of not measuring up. In order to break the grip of such fear (which leads to envy), we can each determine that our pursuits need not depend on the way others conduct themselves. Instead, our behaviors and goals are determined from an inward drive that is based on a genuine desire to please God.

Learn the Joy of Giving

At its root, envy is a selfish emotion concerned about *my* wants, *my* wishes. Replacing this attitude with a giving spirit can go a long way in reversing one's inner drive. Giving produces a feeling of joy based on happiness brought to others. It involves an outpouring of oneself with the specific intent of bringing pleasure into another's life.

In order to control envy, we will seek to give more than just physical items or tangible gifts; we will give intangibles such as genuine praise, understanding, support, and unselfish enthusiasm when success is experienced by another.

Elizabeth, is a good example of a woman with an envy-free heart: "I never have had many expensive things and I guess you could say I've never been a social standout. But my life is really full. I work with young children all day, most of whom come from broken homes. I feel that I have something to give them that really adds to their lives. When I hug one of those youngsters and get hugged in return, I feel like I'm the luckiest person around." Elizabeth's lifestyle was dedicated to making little ones happy, and that was more than enough for her.

Seek Heavenly Things

Envious people on a never-ending search for the good life are seeking things which are earthly and temporal, and their discontent is assured since nothing this world has to offer will last forever.

Colossians 3:1 says: "If then you have been raised up with Christ: keep seeking the things above." And a few verses later "Let the word of Christ richly dwell within you, with all wisdom teaching and admonishing one another with psalms and hymns and spiritual songs, singing with thankfulness in your hearts to God" (v. 16).

The most certain way to resist envy is to become mentally focused on a higher plane. God's word repeatedly teaches that He has a plan for each of us, and His plan transcends matters of this world. Setting our sights on His perfect will, is the surest way to set aside envy and live with a song in our hearts.

Questions for Further Thought

What are the highest priorities in my life: temporal things, or gifts that God has made available to anyone who will seek after Him?

When I see someone else who has experienced gain or success, how can I demonstrate my shared joy?

How do I tend to be status conscious? Why do I have difficulty accepting the fact that the world's idea of greatness does not always coincide with God's?

When do I tend to focus on my rights and needs to the extent that I become self-oriented?

Am I willing to love myself in my present circumstances, just as God loves me?

Which gifts does God make available to anyone who will seek after Him?

5

Grief

We spend a large part of our lives trying to make gains. So it is only natural when losses come, we will have varying emotional reactions. The greater the loss, the greater the emotion will be.

Grief *is the emotion that most often accompanies loss. It is a feeling of anguish, sorrow, or longing for the person or thing that is gone; regret over something done or unfulfilled. Grief can also be accompanied by other feelings such as reminiscing, anger, disillusionment, self-pity, or guilt. More than just a singular emotion, grief often causes a person to sort through many thoughts, feelings, and questions.*

When we think of grief, we often have a mental image of a graveside scene or of a dark, somber hospital room because grief is most often associated with death and illness. But grief is a natural reaction to any loss, such as a loss of a marriage through divorce, the loss of a job, of a friendship, or of a dream. The way we emotionally adjust to such losses is crucial to our personal stability.

Case Study

Carolyn had difficulty handling losses of any kind. So naturally grief was a most difficult emotion for her. As she told me about her life, I realized that she had legitimate reasons to grieve. Several years earlier, as a young wife, she had a miscarriage in the second trimester of her pregnancy. This is an emotionally draining experience for any young woman and grief was a natural response for her. But Carolyn used the event to cut off her fellowship with God and to harbor deep, long-term feelings of dejection. As years passed, Carolyn's bitterness increased whenever she heard of another woman who suffered the same fate. Carolyn's grief reactions were so strong that she did not have control over this emotion and its resulting problems.

Tom lost his wife of twenty-two years and was naturally distraught over losing his lifelong companion. But his grief dominated him. Four years after his wife's death, he vowed that he would never remarry because he wouldn't set himself up for a repetition of the same problem.

People who are uninformed about grief tend to respond differently (often more inappropriately) than people who are aware of the nature of grief. We can prepare ourselves to work through grief properly when times of losses come. Uncontrolled, unresolved grief can lead to widespread emotional problems with feelings of depression, loneliness, and bitterness.

Manifestations of Grief

A State of Shock

When a loss occurs, shock is a common first reaction, demonstrated by statements of disbelief: "I never thought this would happen" or "This isn't what I expected" or "Isn't there anything that can be done about it?" In this initial stage of grief, one hardly knows how to behave, perhaps wanting to talk about it or to cry, but being unable. There is usually a feeling of unreality; numbness to the world around. This feeling can last for a few hours or even several days.

People express shock differently. For example, one person who grieves over being laid off from work may instantly feel the need to talk with someone, while another person may want to be left alone; one person who has lost his home in a violent storm may have a blank stare on his face, while another may have excessive energy. One person who has lost a relative may smile and talk of heaven, while another may cry uncontrollably. There is no one predictable way the shock experience will be exhibited. Certainly shock is a ready response in most cases of grief.

Emotional Release

As the fact of the loss soaks in, a welling up of emotions occurs. The person begins to face the reality that things are not as they were. At this point, tears can readily flow. Anguish reaches its peak and with little or no warning overwhelms the individual. He will probably feel very broken and weak.

The stage of emotional release is an extremely important part of the grief process. Emotional expressions in times of loss must not be repressed lest the individual suffer more painful repercussions at a later date. In the tiny verse "Jesus wept" (John 11:35), we see that even the Master allowed Himself the freedom to express His sorrow over the death of His close friend.

Case Study

Forty-year-old Rowena told me how twenty years earlier her son died soon after he was born. When this heartrending event occurred, she was told by family and friends that she had no reason to weep or feel sorry, because God would take charge of her problem. So Rowena kept her hurt to herself. When she was in my office one day she told me something that reminded her of her baby's death. Without warning she broke down in tears, sobbing deeply and uncontrollably. As she cried, she repeatedly said, "I'm sorry, I'm sorry." I responded with silence and let her cry as long as she needed.

When she recovered, I merely said: "Your feelings run very deep; it must feel good to be able to cry."

With that, she began crying again. Eventually, we were able to talk about her experience. Rowena said: "No one has ever let me show my emotions like this. I can't tell you how cleansed I feel right now."

The next week Rowena told me how she had shared her grief with her husband. "Les, you wouldn't believe it," she said. "My husband did the same thing I did in your office. We both got our emotions out and we talked about our lost baby for the first time in twenty years and felt a real sense of healing!"

Twenty years! How much better their lives would have been if they'd expressed their grief right away.

I can assure you, the longer the emotions are repressed, the more difficult they can be to "sort out" when they finally surface. Allow such emotions to surface at the first opportunity.

Feelings of Loneliness and Isolation

Several years ago I suffered a severe accident that put me in the hospital for eight weeks. I required seven operations over a period of two years, and had to make adjustments in my previous physical activities: no more tennis, less endurance, etc. You can imagine that during my time of adjustment, grief was a prominent emotional issue for me. During my time of recuperation there was one phrase that people would say to me that would send me up the wall. Countless times I heard folks say: "I know how you must feel." Instantly, I would think to myself, irritably: "No you don't; how could you?"

You see, part of my grief was being in my own lonely, isolated world. I had no idea how I was going to handle my personal loss, so how could anyone possibly say that they understood me? Even I didn't always understand me! Besides, none of them had gone through what I had.

With grief, a feeling of isolation is natural. It is common to assume that no one else knows the same feeling. There is a desire to reach out and become significantly connected with friends and family, but it is difficult to fully share one's feelings and to accept another's comfort as being genuine. This sense of isolation is normal and is most likely to become prominent after the initial shock and flow of emotion has waned. Knowing this, the grieving person can rest assured that this feeling will not be completely dominant for an indefinite period of time.

Guilt Feelings

When a person experiences loss of a relative to death, a dating relationship, material possessions, etc., that individual can become an easy target for guilt. He tries to analyze what went wrong, to figure out what could have been done differently. With hindsight it is always easier to pinpoint flaws. And one's guilt quickly gets out of proportion.

For example, a surviving family member or friend of a deceased person will endlessly ruminate about not having expressed enough love to that person. Or a parent grieves over a child's failure, asking, "Where did we go wrong?" Or a person suffers significant financial loss and questions judgments made. For example, a woman's husband declared bankruptcy, and a month later died suddenly of a heart attack. She agonized over what she should have done to prevent both her husband's financial problems and his unexpected death.

It is crucial that a person learns to distinguish between true guilt and false guilt. There are times when a person can evaluate past failures in an effort to make positive, constructive resolutions about the future. True guilt is at work in that assessment because it leads to repentance and renewal. False guilt involves a mental scolding of self that leads the individual to feel a sense of lowered value and worth, and also to long-term struggles.

Anger and Disillusionment

Eventually the grieving individual experiences anger and disillusionment. Efforts have been made to let go of the person or thing lost. Feelings of sadness have been expressed. Questions about the past have been mulled over and the final reality of the loss is recognized. Now the use of anger becomes an extremely delicate issue. It can be expressed in a way that allows feelings to be ventilated and released, or it can be nurtured to the extent that long-term bitterness results.

One man who had a terminal disease experienced anger as part of the grief process accompanying his impending death. For several weeks he had tried to adjust (successfully, he thought) to the fact that his days literally were numbered. He shared sad moments with his family and reminisced for hours about his past. Seemingly, he had come to terms with his fate. But late one night, a nurse entered his hospital room to take his blood pressure. The man jerked his arm from her grasp and angrily said: "Leave me alone! Go away!" This startled the nurse, so she left. It also startled the patient. Later, a chaplain assured him that such a reaction was not at all unusual. He counseled him, though, to examine his anger and not let it turn into a resentment that would hurt himself and others.

When a loss occurs, a period of a prominent, critical, negative (angry) mind-set is inevitable. For example, an angry patient may scrutinize his doctor's every move. A surviving spouse may become angry with God for allowing an untimely death. Or a college student may become angry at "the way people are insensitive" when a long-term dating relationship ends. It is important for the grieving individual to allow himself to be angry while at the same time recognizing the need to keep it from becoming permanently fixed.

How to Control Grief

Case Study

"My family life is coming apart at the seams," Ruth told me. "Ever since my husband's death we have had nothing but problems." Ruth explained that three months ago her husband had died of heart failure. She and her two grown sons were constantly at odds with one another because each had such differing reactions to his death. Ruth had significant struggles with guilt as she reminded herself that she could have been a better wife during their thirty-seven years together. Her oldest son was openly hostile about his father's death because he and the father had been laying the groundwork for a new family business. But now, this son's hopes were dashed. The younger son, however, seemed to be perturbed at both his mother and brother because he felt they should just put the past behind and go on with life. That's what he personally was trying to do, so he assumed they should, too.

Naturally, when mother and sons got together for visits (they all lived in the same town), their discussions would readily turn sour. Each was handling grief in a different way.

Can you see how easily the grief process can get out of hand? Since grief elicits such a broad range of reactions, confusion can reign supreme. Several key techniques to help us maintain our senses even as our emotions are troubled with grief are listed below.

Allow for Unpredictable Changes in Emotions

Most of us like to have a fair amount of predictability in life. For instance, we work hard to establish family security and financial security. We like the predictability of having familiar routines. We look for ways to carve out a niche in the way we interact with business associates, friends, neighbors, family, church members, etc. We are creatures of habit. When an unexpected loss occurs, our whole predictable, secure foundation is shaken. Plans need to be altered. Routines are changed. Old friendly acquaintances may no longer be a part of one's life. New people enter our lives. Uncomfortable, difficult decisions must be made. One's feelings resemble a tossed salad.

Make allowance for the fact that emotions can come and go, sometimes without explanation. For example, there will be times when you feel calm, only to be interrupted by an unexplained sense of panic. Or perhaps you may be speaking with a friend, and you find yourself fighting off seemingly irrational feelings of depression.

Although grief has usually similar accompanying experiences it is by no means a completely predictable emotion. Rather than becoming alarmed, accept this unpredictability as the norm.

Turn your Eyes Toward God

When we experience loss, we very easily focus on God. Some individuals are very cynical and angry, questioning God's wisdom, His timing, His kindness. Others, however, seek to draw strength from Him, and rely on His guidance for the future. Because we have some inner notions about God, we look to Him in our own way at times of crisis. Our prior beliefs about Him will determine if our thoughts and feelings will be constructive or destructive.

Many people ask, "Why do bad things have to happen?" This is a good question to ask because it forces us to grapple with the reality of sin. As we struggle with the reasons behind our losses, we come to recognize that our world is sin-stained and imperfect. It has many pleasures to offer, but everything touched by humanity is blemished. This explains why losses occur. This explains death. Because of our sins, we will experience physical death and will be susceptible to other losses such as a devastated marriage, dashed hopes, or personal tragedies. We don't like to face this truth, yet face it we must.

But the beauty that follows the acknowledgment of our sin is the blessed assurance that God actively pursues us to save us from our sins, and mercifully provides avenues that lead to solace and peace. In other words, though we experience grief in our lives because of our imperfect nature, we can turn to a God who understands our needs and who has already paved the way toward a life of fulfillment. In this way grief can be used to put us in direct contact with His love. In our times of sorrow, we should be willing to ask questions about God ("How long, O Lord, wilt thou quite forget me? . . . How long must I suffer anguish in my soul?" Ps. 13:1a, 2a, NEB). But we must also then be willing to search His Word to learn all we can about the grace and power He offers ("If you call to me I will answer you, and tell you great and mysterious things which you do not understand" Jer. 33:2b, NEB; "Do you not know? Have you not heard? The Lord is the everlasting God, the Creator of the ends of the earth. He will not grow tired or weary, and his understanding no one can fathom. He gives strength to the weary and increases the power of the weak" Isa. 40:28–29).

Hold on to Hope and Look Forward to the Future

One manifestation of grief is a loss of hope. Grief can cause a person to assume that the future is bleak, containing no hope of eventual joy.

While it is easy and normal for grieving people to experience periodic bouts with hopelessness, the Bible encourages us not to fall completely to defeat. The psalmist wrote: "My hope is from Him. He only is my rock and my salvation, my stronghold; I shall not be shaken" (Ps. 62:5–6). We are promised that there is no tribulation that God will allow to completely overwhelm us; He is always willing to give us whatever strength is needed for our circumstances (see 1 Cor. 10:13). In the most famous psalm we are assured: "Even though I walk through the valley of the shadow of death, I fear no evil; for Thou art with me; Thy rod and Thy staff, they comfort me" (Ps. 23:4).

Repeatedly, God's Word assures us that we have a reason to hold on to hope because of His guiding hand. I am convinced that those who have a strong faith in God's sovereignty will be able to successfully complete the grieving process because, knowing that God has always provided for past needs, these people are able to trust in His consistency, and have faith that He will also provide for the future.

Have you ever noticed how children can worry about their problems to the extent that they can work themselves into a feeling of hopelessness? For example, the school child may feel hopelessly worried about going into a new classroom, or perhaps the toddler is afraid of the dark. Usually, when these kinds of situations arise, we adults smile knowingly and encourage our children to proceed in spite of their hopeless feelings. We know from experience that their obstacles are not overwhelming.

In the same way, God encourages us to proceed when losses occur. Though we feel burdened by hopelessness, He knows that we have more ability and endurance than we sometimes realize. In faith we can follow His urging and move into the future, knowing that He will always give us the tools needed for contentment.

Stay in Touch with Routine Matters

When we go through the process of grief, there are two extremes to be avoided: (1) blocking out feelings altogether in an effort to pretend that everything is perfectly fine, and (2) being so totally consumed with emotions that nothing else matters. Emotional balance is the most healthy course, particularly as more and more time passes by. It is quite proper to let our emotions have their day, but it is also healing to gradually work ourselves back into the world of routines.

Case Study

Charlie, in his mid-twenties, was just reaching the peak of his physical abilities when he suffered a car accident that left him paralyzed from his waist down. He went through months and months of agony and turmoil. But once he began accepting the permanence of his paralysis, Charlie acknowledged his need to get his life back on track. He still had a career to pursue, so he slowly worked his way back into his work routine. He and his wife renewed social contacts and again became involved in their church. Charlie's emotions began to heal and his hurt receded as he got back into the "world of the living" again.

Since grief is an emotion connected with losses, a way to bring completion to grief is to eventually reposition oneself so gains can again be pursued and resolution to one's grief can take place. A first step in this process is for the grieving individual to move back into the flow of normal social interaction.

How to Respond to Another Person's Grief

"When someone else is experiencing grief, what should I do?" The answer is complicated because people handle grief differently. Some people will want to be left alone, while others want constant companionship. Some will want words of comfort, while others would prefer silence. Responding to another's grief is a delicate matter.

While there are no hard and fast rules, the following suggestions may assist you in helping another person through the grieving process.

Be Available

Be available when loss comes to a friend or loved one. This doesn't necessarily mean camping out at that person's doorstep, but it does involve a consistent checking on the needs of the grieving person. So often, when another person is troubled, one's words are not nearly as important as one's presence.

Case Study

Kay's friend's husband suffered a severe accident. This woman had no nearby relatives, so Kay spent many hours with the troubled wife. Kay felt badly, though, because she knew she wasn't a good conversationalist and she felt unable to fully communicate her concern. Yet Kay's worries evaporated when a couple of weeks later she received a warm "thank you" note from her friend. "I don't know how I could have made it through Jim's surgery without you. What a sacrifice you made to stay with me all through the night when no one else was there! I felt I could always call on you knowing that I have a friend who really cares." Kay realized it was her availability, not her words, that impressed her friend.

Think about a friend who was kind to you several years ago. What do you remember most about that person? Likely, it's not the person's specific words and deeds, but his presence and sensitivity to your needs.

Be Adaptive in Your Communication Style

Be aware that people handle grief in different ways. One family member may have countless questions; another may crave solitude. When you visit a grieving individual, be willing to "go with" the communication needs of that person.

A minister friend told me about a recent visit with a young couple in shock due to the sudden death of the young husband's sister. Both were having a hard time sorting through their feelings.

The minister walked into a quiet, tense living room. Both husband and wife were silent; few words were exchanged. After the pastor shared some words of comfort, he said a prayer, and made his way to the front door. The husband accompanied him outside and showered him with a myriad of questions. He had so many things on his mind that they talked for over an hour in the front yard. When the minister finally left, he realized that the silence in the living room was caused by the wife's desire to sort out her feelings in quiet. But the husband's needs were different, and they also needed to be met.

Ask grieving individuals discreet questions about their circumstances and feelings. In fact, it can be a helpful icebreaker to outwardly acknowledge the loss and to seek information. But once you've shown a genuine interest, let the grieving one direct the course of conversation. If you get little or no response, don't push the issue. Take it as a sign that silence is needed.

Several months ago I visited a man hospitalized with a brain tumor. I sensed that he wanted to share the medical details with me. But when I asked him to tell me about the tumor, another visitor (obviously uncomfortable with the situation) quickly injected: "Don't worry him with those kinds of things, let him get his rest." Clearly, the other visitor was imposing his communication style on both me and our sick friend. When the visitor left, my sick friend said: "Thank you for asking about my condition. Everyone seems to be treating me like a child." We had a good discussion about his problem. More importantly, my suffering friend felt free to handle his feelings in his own way.

Don't Use Pat Responses

Probably the greatest irritant to a grieving individual is statements such as, "I know how you must feel." "Don't worry, things will get better." Any recently grieving person can readily rattle off a dozen of these little ditties offered by well-meaning souls.

Why are pat answers so aggravating? They are used so frequently that they lose their meaning and become little more than empty phrases. Consequently, they have an impersonal feel. And impersonal words are the last thing a person needs at a time when sensitivities are extremely high.

It is more helpful to offer a grieving person empathy, support, and genuine encouragement. An honest admission of your inability to precisely understand the situation is in order. Nothing could be more comforting than: "At a time like this it's hard for me to fully appreciate what you must be feeling. But I want you to know of my love for you and my availability." There is no need to put on pretenses. Honest expressions are more helpful than superficial platitudes.

Sometimes words may not be needed at all. At peak times of loss, people often are not interested in what others think. A friend's presence, a hug, and a few tears can be more valuable than words. Your offer of assistance in mundane chores or just your physical presence can be the most touching communication.

Be in Prayer for the Grieving Person

In times of bereavement, an individual usually has more intense spiritual thoughts than normal, whether in the form of increased dependence on God or of increased questioning of God. Consequently, an encourager can be of great assistance by praying about the situation, giving spiritual help at a time when this dimension is heightened. Praying may be done with the grieving person, either aloud or silently, or it may be done apart from the person. Since the Holy Spirit acts as the Comforter, He is available and desires to play a role in the lives of the disheartened. The grieving person may be prompted to seek God. The power of prayer must not be overlooked. Matthew 11:28 sums this up beautifully: "Come to Me, all who are weary and heavy-laden, and I will give you rest."

Questions for Further Thought

When I encounter grief, how do I allow myself to experience the wide range of emotions that accompany it? Or do I keep tight, rigid control over myself?

When others grieve how do I show understanding in the way I relate to their grief? Am I honest with them?

How do I see loss as a motivation to depend more on God?

What is hope? What is my hope? How do I hold on to hope in the midst of very trying situations? Can I believe that God will be of utmost assistance to me?

6

Guilt

A well-known minister tells the story of a man who came to him desperately seeking peace of mind. The man began by sharing experiences from a period of his life that kept bringing haunting memories. This man was a former soldier who had spent several months in the South Pacific during World War II. Though it had been years since his discharge, his mind was tormented with guilt.

In sharing his story he revealed that he and a group of fellow soldiers had made a solemn vow to "kill every Jap possible"; they had even gone so far to draw their own blood and taste it as a token of their commitment to this agreement. Subsequently, their pact led them to seek and destroy the enemy, not as an act of war, but as an act of cold-hearted vicious murder. On several occasions Japanese soldiers offered to surrender as prisoners of war. Their testimony would have been invaluable to military intelligence. But instead of being humane, these men shot the enemy soldiers summarily with no sense of compassion. While the helpless men had pleaded for mercy, the self-appointed band of assassins remained true to their vow to kill.

As the years passed, this former soldier went through spells of anguish in which he would awaken at night, soaked in his own sweat. He had persistent nightmares reliving those days filled with unrelenting hate. He would see the faces of pitiable men begging him to let them live another day. In public, he sank in shame whenever an Oriental person walked by.

As he spoke with the minister, this man (who was by now a well-respected pillar of the business community) shared that it was virtually impossible to comprehend how God could forgive him of his past crimes. When he heard the words "God loves you" he cringed in remorse because he felt he had no redeeming value. He had become so introspective and withdrawn that any interactions beyond the most superficial level were too stressful. He was in such a state of agony that he could not possibly forgive himself.

Like this man, many people have been driven to the depths of despair because of a lingering sense of guilt. In this calendar year over twenty-five thousand people will drop to such a low point that they will end it all by taking their own lives. Thousands more will try but will not succeed. The emotion of guilt can be a great destroyer.

Few of us will actually suffer guilt to this extreme, but all of us are troubled occasionally by the recurring aches of unresolved memories. When left unchecked, this guilt can stunt emotional growth. It can produce all sorts of hang-ups that cut deeply into one's self-image, and it can deepen into depression or rebellion and loneliness.

How are we to handle guilt? When it arises should we ignore it, repress it, confess it? What are we to do?

First, we need to get an understanding of the different facets of guilt. Although some guilt can be totally debilitating, this emotion is given to us for positive reasons. Originally God gave it to mankind to serve the redemptive purpose of bringing all individuals into right fellowship with Him. Through guilt we are each challenged to come to grips with the sense of right and wrong established by God. In both His written Word and in each person's sense of conscience, God reveals the basic laws of morality and truth and exhorts individuals to draw close to Him. Just as physical pain communicates that something is amiss in one's body, guilt can communicate that all is not right in one's style of living and thinking. It is important to understand that there are the two kinds of guilt:

1. True guilt *is the constructive feeling of remorse based on a reasonable understanding of God's standard of right and wrong.* For example, when a person tells a lie he feels guilty. Inwardly he knows that he has violated one of God's directives. Therefore, because of his sense of regret, he atones for his error, making the necessary corrections. True guilt is the inner voice that instructs the individual to choose right over wrong. It is this emotion that leads a person to live a life of moral responsibility.

Encouraging Christians to respond to the inner sense of right and wrong, the apostle Paul wrote: "Test yourself to see if you are in the faith; examine yourselves" (2 Cor. 13:5). An emotional and a mental reaction to God's directives can help Christians gain a sense of morality that brings honor to Him. True guilt is therefore the emotion that causes an individual to take stock productively of his innermost thoughts and attitudes and the behavior that results.

2. False guilt *is a feeling of remorse that assumes a judgmental posture toward oneself (note that judging is entirely different from examining oneself). False guilt involves a subjective condemnation in light of the fact that a wrong has been committed.* Attached to false guilt is the fear of being found out and the fear of receiving harsh punishment. This type of guilt usually has negative repercussions because it hinders a person from accepting the fullness of God's forgiveness. The experience of false guilt is inappropriate because it encourages a person to feel that he has no value because of personal sins.

Notice the differences between true guilt and false guilt. Whereas true guilt causes a person to draw closer to God, false guilt creates a sense of isolation or estrangement from Him. True guilt brings improvement to a person's life; false guilt causes life to lose its joy. True guilt produces a humble, repentant spirit; false guilt produces feelings of defeat and degradation.

Reactions to Guilt

There is a variety of ways in which people respond to guilt. At times it is a constructive emotion that produces positive changes in a person. At other times it festers in the mind causing damaging anguish and torment. There are times when the individual simply ignores guilt as if it didn't even exist. Of course, this usually leads to problems.

Case Study

John was a man in his early thirties whose life could best be described as a kind of rollercoaster ride. He had grown up in an average-home atmosphere. There was a little turmoil in his family, but nothing abnormal. John says that when he left home for college he was ready to try any and all new experiences. He allowed himself to become involved in promiscuity, alcohol abuse, and cheating schemes. And, as he describes it, he felt little guilt over his misdeeds; he was choosing to ignore God's order of right and wrong.

But things changed when John left college for a career in real estate. He met a Christian woman who took him to church and eventually helped him understand his need for salvation. At twenty-six, John became a Christian. At first, his Christian experience was a pure joy. He felt that a whole new way of life had opened to him. For a while he felt a peace he had never before experienced. But in time, John became troubled when he realized he still had old sinful tendencies residing in him. On the outside it seemed that he had a solid grasp on the fulfilled life, but inwardly he knew that in an enticing environment, he could potentially revert to his past ways.

A gnawing sense of unworthiness grew inside John. He began to feel shame because of his inner weaknesses. A sense of uncleanness overwhelmed him. Gradually he began to draw away from his church fellowship. He quit praying and reading his Bible. He told his wife he was sorry that he had ever become a Christian. "If being a Christian means that I can't stand myself because of all my faults, I don't want to have anything to do with it." His knowledge of right and wrong had led directly to the self-degrading false guilt. A close friend noticed the turmoil in John and by counseling with him was able to stop his downward spiral. This friend helped John see that he needed to shift his focus. John needed to concentrate less on how bad he was and more on how much God loved him. The friend was correct in advising John to take advantage of the constructive nature of guilt for motivating moral responsibility and avoiding reversion to his old life-style.

Causes of False Guilt

Some people live with gnawing guilt for so long they develop patterns that only perpetuate it in a negative way. Once they sink into the mire of false guilt, they tend to stay there. There are several patterns that cause this inappropriate emotion to proceed harmfully.

A Narrow Perspective of God's Love

I once talked with a woman who had assumed all her life that God was a stern taskmaster. She envisioned Him as an angry dictator who spent His time keeping account of all the wrongs committed by people. In fact, in her childhood she had been so fearful of God's harsh rebuke that she used to make small fires in her backyard and hold her hands as close to the fire as she could bear. She was so sure of God's eventual rejection that she was trying to prepare herself for the fires of hell.

I cannot count the people I have talked with who suffered endlessly in crippling guilt because of a limited picture of the love of God. They assume that God is predominantly a condemner because they see that *people* are quick to condemn. In their narrow thinking, they humanize God. Instead of seeing Him as a God who wants fellowship with humans and who is willing to be forgiving, guilt-laden people picture Him as one who is critical as any mortal creature might be. This mindset makes inappropriate guilt inevitable.

A Poor Self-Image

Within the human personality, self-image is the foundation upon which all emotions are based. You might say that self-image is the hub of the wheel. When an individual has a perception of self that is consistent with God's love for each human, that person will be able to respond to guilt in a constructive fashion. But when one's self-image is negative and derogatory, false guilt will abound.

One man explained it this way: "I have always been conditioned to think lowly of myself. To me, self-love is the same as arrogance and conceit. Naturally when I do something wrong my negative thinking increases. I just can't seem to get away from the feeling that I'm no good. I always seem to be judging myself."

Rather than grasping the fact of God's love, an individual with a negative self-image makes his own judgment of himself. This creates a sense of insecurity and clouds his mental abilities to sort through guilt in the constructive manner intended by God.

Chronic Critical Thinking

We all know what it is like to be judged and evaluated; it is a part of life. But some people hold so tightly to their judgmental attitude that they compulsively toss out one criticism after another. When people spend a lot of mental energy in self-criticism, they become extremely vulnerable to false guilt. They are often unable to differentiate between critiquing, or analyzing, their behavior to objectively determine right from wrong and criticizing their behavior with an implied condemnation.

Case Study

Gaye had this problem. In her childhood she had received many lectures about right and wrong. Yet she had little direction in the matter of a wholesome sense of self-worth. Therefore, it was only natural for her to assume that when she did something wrong she could expect a critical rebuke; it would automatically "prove" how bad she was. False guilt was the predominant emotion of life. In her adult years she cringed whenever she made a mistake. She was highly sensitive to her personal flaws. She put constant pressure on herself to be a supermom, but she never felt that she measured up. When I talked with her about the need to *examine* her flaws without *judging* herself, she was befuddled. A critical mindset was so natural to her that anything else seemed abnormal.

The person with a critical thought pattern has a hard time distinguishing between corrective admonishing and destructive shame. There is little room for forgiveness.

Over-Identifying with Rules

False guilt is also promoted by relating all behavior to rules and regulations. Obligation is the name of the game. In an effort to bring predictability and security into one's life, it is easy simply to make a rule for everything. However, relating to the world primarily through a list of rules potentially leads to psychological stress.

Do you remember who clashed most often with Jesus during His earthly ministry? It was the Pharisees. Those guys had an unbelievable list of regulations hanging over their heads. They could hardly make a decision without consulting the rule book. To say they were rigid is an understatement. Condemnation was quick for anyone who ever broke one of their sacred rules—and no one was exempt. Even Jesus Christ became the object of their scorn.

One incident that demonstrated the hollow harshness of the Pharisees occurred when Jesus healed a man with a withered hand on the Sabbath (Mark 3:1–6). To prove a point Jesus performed His miracle on the Sabbath, and they were unable to perceive the good because of their regulations. Because of their hang-ups regarding the rules the Pharisees attempted to produce false guilt in Jesus, but He was not susceptible.

Obviously, the nit-picky legalism of the Pharisees doesn't exist now in the same way it did two thousand years ago. Yet we all have known people who create false guilt, either in themselves or in others, because of their stubborn holding fast to the rule book. While God intended that His biblical directives to be positive encouragers to show a sinful world how to get right with Him, many have taken them to be negative reinforcers for vile people.

Controlling Guilt

Our goal is *not* to live guilt-free. As long as we are sinners, we need to have our consciences pricked to keep our behavior and attitudes in line with God's will. Our goal is to learn how to *control* our guilt so it does not turn sour and lead to condemnation and self-induced misery. Fortunately, there are some guidelines for keeping guilt under proper control.

Acknowledging God's Love

When people fall into a pattern of false guilt their main mental focus is on failure. They see themselves as irresponsible and unworthy before God. So they convince themselves that they do not deserve forgiveness and love. They accept false guilt, and its condemnation, as their just reward.

The truth is that no human is really deserving of the love of God. We all have fallen so low because of our sins that death is the payoff we should receive. But deserving or not, God wills to love us. Even though we deserve death, He repeatedly offers new life. "For the wages of sin is death, but the free gift of God is eternal life in Christ Jesus our Lord" (Rom. 6:23). God chooses to give us His love freely in spite of ourselves. This is a fact that sin does not change.

The Bible discusses our sinful nature frequently and in great detail, but it also repeatedly gives the message that *all* humans are important to God. Genesis 1:26–27 says that mankind was created as the crowning pinnacle of all creation, in the very image of God, for the purpose of having dominion over all the earth. This theme is reiterated in other biblical passages. First Corinthians 11:7 refers to the Corinthian Christians (who had terrible moral struggles) as being "the image and glory of God." James 3:9 encourages us to speak kindly to one another since we "are made in the likeness of God."

The unmistakable fact is that even when we have gone to the very depths of sin, we are still extremely valuable to God! Our dignity and value may not be high in the eyes of other humans, but the One whose opinion counts says that we are supremely treasured. Consequently, rather than having failure as our *main* focus, we can concentrate on receiving the love God desires to give each of us.

Understanding God's Punishment

Guilt-laden people sometimes say, "God, I wish you would just go ahead and punish me and get it over with!" I want to counter such a plea with the suggestion that if you are a Christian, God will never punish you. Many people may shake their heads in disbelief at such a thought. But it is true. According to Romans 8:1, "There is therefore now no condemnation for those who are in Christ Jesus." God punishes no Christian. He *disciplines* us, but He does not punish, and there is a tremendous difference between the two.

Punishment is the payment for sins. All sinners deserve the death sentence as punishment for defiance against God, but since Jesus Christ paid the price of that punishment for us on the cross, our debt has been completely paid. All who call upon the name of Jesus as their Savior and Master have been freed from their deserved punishment forevermore. Because the death of Jesus on the cross was sufficient, you and I as Christians never need to fear the punishment of God.

Discipline is quite different from punishment. It has a teaching purpose. It is meant to bring the individual back to the original purpose for which he was created. It has a positive goal, though it may not be pleasant at the time. This is why *true* guilt is a gift to us. God has placed in our consciences a distinct ability to respond to right and wrong. It is part of His masterplan for revealing His love.

Just as a parent disciplines a child for the purpose of preparing him for a well-ordered life, so God disciplines His children. By means of discipline He brings us to maturity. Discipline is future-oriented, while punishment is past-oriented. That is, God's discipline serves to instruct us in ways to live more effectively for Him in the days to come, whereas punishment reflects God's wrath toward past deeds.

God usually disciplines us through the laws of consequence and of conscience. For example, when a person abuses the body by filling it with excessive amounts of alcohol, the consequence is the loss of some normal bodily and mental functions. Also the person is likely to experience the negative reinforcement of a hangover. This law of consequence was placed in motion by God who wishes to teach His children that it is best to take care of their earthly bodies.

The person who acts in an unkind or irresponsible manner toward a family member is prone to feel uneasiness of mind and pangs of conscience until the matter is resolved. This is also an instance of negative reinforcement given by the God of love who knows that His subjects need to be guided back into right living.

As you learn to distinguish between God's punishment and His discipline, you will understand that He wants the very best for us. He does not want us to tremble in self-condemnation when we do wrong; He wants us to respect Him and acknowledge the perfection of His ways.

The Purpose of Rules

Many people who suffer from false guilt are hung up on rules. When they catch themselves breaking a rule, they are apt to condemn themselves to the point of self-rejection. They have taken something useful, a rule, and turned it into a burden.

It is true, of course, that we need biblical rules for guidance and direction, but we need to determine the best way to use these rules so that they give us useful boundaries without stifling and oppressing us with guilt. The following guidelines can lead to a positive use of rules and regulations.

First, rules are needed to strengthen the individual, not to make one feel worthless.

Second, rules remind one that a life patterned on appropriate and responsible behavior has advantages over one that is loose and undisciplined. In this sense, rules encourage us to be goal-oriented.

Third, rules lead the Christian to experience contentment in life. They are meant to show the way to success, not failure.

Fourth, rules give us concrete instructions for giving God due honor and glory. God has made us for relationship with Him, and He has carefully spelled out how we can best go about it.

Once we understand the constructive nature of God's rules we gain a broader perspective of His love for us. God has no desire to make people grovel in lowly feelings about themselves. He provides all possible avenues to lead us to a fulfilled life.

Healthful Repentance

So far we have considered how false guilt can be controlled by mentally focusing on God's love and understanding the purpose of His discipline and rules. This should enable us to set aside the self-judgmental attitude of false guilt. But this does not mean that the person experiencing true guilt will have no emotional reaction at all. There will be strong emotion attached to true guilt; it is not a process of detached mechanical reasoning.

"Godly sorrow brings repentance that leads to salvation and leaves no regret" (2 Cor. 7:10, NIV). This means that when a person recognizes the error of his ways, he need not wail and moan in self-degrading regret, yet there will be a genuine sadness. Paul refers to it as sorrow with repentance. A Christian who commits sin will have an emotional reaction of sadness, but it is sadness that is beneficial.

Case Study

I have a close friend, Dave, who is one of the finest Christians I know. He has many spiritual gifts, including evangelism, comforting, encouraging, which he puts to constant use for the Lord. To see him in action you would think that he had had special training and a strong Christian background to be such an on-fire witness, but that is not the case.

Dave accepted Christ just a few short years ago when in his mid-thirties. Before that he was a self-centered, angry man. He was impulsive in his decisions and manipulative in his relationships. As he himself says, he could not have cared less about God, but one day a business associate set him down and explained to him the need for salvation. The friend showed such a concern for him that Dave was deeply moved. In the days that followed Dave spent hours thinking about the sins he had committed. As his insights into God's love deepened, so did his sense of true guilt. He prayed with his friend and invited Jesus into his heart. After he was saved, he realized that he would be burdened only if he carried false guilt over his past wrongs. He knew he would not be able to forget the past, so he set himself to learn from it.

Dave explains that when he thinks of his past life of defiance to God, he feels saddened, though not burdened. His sadness has been relieved by a healthy repentance. Because he has no intention of reverting to his former lifestyle, he is motivated by his memories of it to live productively for God.

The difference between repentant sorrow and false guilt lies in the signals sent to the person. False guilt says, "I'm bad." Repentant sorrow says "I will correct the wrongs I've done." False guilt bogs a person down in self-inflicted misery, repentant sorrow leads to positive changes in both attitude and behavior.

Humility

When a person responds to guilt in healthy repentance, a sense of humility is the result. The guilty person will readily admit that he truly deserves the wrath of God, but when he realizes God's desire and willingness to forgive no matter how great the sin, there is a feeling of unrestrained gladness. There is no place for gloating or pride when a person properly resolves the guilt in a sinful life, rather, there is the warm inner comfort and security that results from being loved and forgiven by God the Creator.

Once a woman who had been caught in the act of adultery was brought before Jesus by the Pharisees (John 8:1–11), who challenged him to decide her fate according to the law of Moses. Would He let her be stoned as commanded, or would He let her go? Jesus responded by saying, "He who is without sin among you, let him be the first to throw a stone at her." Of course, this spoiled the trap the Pharisees had laid for Him, and they went away. Once the crowd was gone the woman stood silently in front of Jesus. He could have scolded her for her sin, reminding her of how wicked she was. This approach would have produced false guilt. Instead He gazed at her with love in His eyes and told her He had no condemnation for her. Jesus so loved this woman that He did not let a rule to get in the way of her coming to know Him.

I've often wondered what happened to that woman in the months and years following this encounter. I'm sure that she felt sorrow for the sins of her past, but there is no doubt in my mind that she remained one of Jesus' most loyal followers to the end of her days. Rather than sinking into destructive false guilt, she must have responded to the fact that Jesus chose to lift her to a level of respectability by His love. She would have certainly felt humble about herself, yet she felt special as a child of God.

God wants nothing to get in the way of our knowledge of His love for us. With this in mind, I encourage you to view your guilt as a positive gift given to you to place you back on track in the merciful hands of the Lord.

Questions for Further Thought

Which of my memories need to be put to rest? How can I forgive myself as God has forgiven me?

When do I have a tendency to see God as harsh and punitive? How can I accept His lovingkindness as complete even though I cannot understand such great love?

How do I use rules? What initiates my good actions, a sense of obligation or choice? Why?

What determines my self-image: my performances or the truth that God loves me more than I can ever comprehend?

7

Impatience

The tapping of Dick's foot told me that he was in a fidgety mood. He leaned over to me and whispered, "If this meeting gets any more boring I think I'll die right here on the spot." Just about that time we heard the words, "Meeting's adjourned." Dick hurriedly stood up and made a beeline for the nearest door. But in doing so, he broadsided a petite young lady, knocking her back into her chair, causing him to drop the notebook and folders he was carrying. Papers went flying everywhere, and there was Dick standing in the middle of one big mess, red-faced. His impatience had gotten the best of him.

I write this chapter with a somewhat sheepish smile and with the feeling of being a genuine expert on the subject. Being aggressive and impetuous in the various aspects of my personal and professional life, impatience is a feeling I can speak of from a background of broad experience. I could relate very easily to Dick's overeagerness to get things moving. I suppose anyone who wants things to happen is going to be vulnerable to this feeling.

To illustrate the nature of this emotion let us consider some circumstances that can trigger an impatient reaction. You may be late for an appointment, held back by your children who just don't seem to share your concern for promptness. You may be listening to an acquaintance who talks on and on about those vacation plans, not realizing how truly uninterested you are in his ramblings. You may be facing a deadline at work but are unable to get the job done because you are held up by that oh-so-pokey co-worker. Most of us face circumstances daily that can bring out our impatient side. To say that we need to get a grip on this feeling is an understatement.

While impatience can be felt in a variety of surroundings and exhibited in an array of behaviors, there are some general rules that can help us get a handle on the problem. First, we can each identify the areas in which we are personally vulnerable to impatience. We can also try to understand the underlying reasons for our impatience. Then finally, we can work toward specific solutions to curtail it.

Impatience *is a feeling of restlessness that stems from a desire for relief or change. It is an intolerance of something that is hindering a personal goal or preference. It implies an irritable and testy nature. It is the opposite of calm and composure.*

In order to control this emotion, it is helpful to examine ourselves carefully. A first step might be to identify personal traits that make us highly susceptible to this feeling.

 1 Time-consciousness; wanting to be prompt; always in a hurry
 2 Heavy use of such words as "should" or "have to"
 3 Preconceived notions of how people should behave
 4 Desire to be influential
 5 Strict in discipline
 6 Single-minded in thought
 7 Insistent in communication practices
 8 Super-stern in rules of morality
 9 Tendency to tune people out; to be preoccupied
10 Tend to be self-centered
11 Frustrated when things don't go as planned
12 Intent to be well organized
13 Inner struggle with anger
14 Have a stubborn streak
15 Exhibit insecurity in social or family relationships
16 Crave freedom; do not want to be tied down
17 Rigid in thought and habit; lacking spontaneity

As you can imagine, impatience arises in many ways and circumstances. One lady's experience describes this well.

Case Study

Pam was the mother of three school-aged children. Before her first child was born she prided herself in being the picture of composure. Even in the often hectic life of a school teacher she was skilled in keeping her cool. "As I look back on those days, I suppose my calmness was due to the fact that I was pretty much in control of my life."

Two brief years into her marriage Pam was delivering the first of her three girls. "I always wanted to be a mother, but I guess I was in for a shock. It was more work than I thought it would be." Seven years and two children later, she was really frazzled. As she described it, she just wasn't the same person as she had been during those school-teaching years. Each day she had such a long list of things-to-do that she seemed to be perpetually behind in her daily routine. She found herself edgy and curt in her disciplinary practices. Her husband described her as bossy and critical ("I never knew this side of her before"). Pam tried to get involved in activities at church but she had a hard time finding pleasure because her mind constantly seemed to be somewhere else. When she was with her friends her conversation tended to take on a negative tone. Moreover, she rarely relaxed; her mind was persistently on other matters. Her entire lifestyle could be described in one word "impatient." Pam needed to slow down, reset priorities, and take time to enjoy activities with her husband and children.

Case Study

As another illustration, consider John. His claim to distinction was that he was his own man. In his late twenties he had broken away from his position in the corporate world and formed his own small business. Through the years he became very successful in his work because he used very sound, logical management procedures. John's motto was If you're going to do something, do it right.

John's problem with impatience stemmed from the fact that he was not able to practice this same work ethic at home. He tried, but he could not persuade his wife and children to live according to the principles that had made his business such a success. He was infuriated if his wife was twenty minutes late for a dinner engagement, and he lost his cool if the children left toys and clothes around in their rooms. "How are we ever going to get anywhere as a family if no one is organized?" He was technically correct in what he wanted his family to achieve, but his impatience caused him to communicate in a self-defeating manner. In fact, things got so bad that John could not contain his emotions for more than a day or two. There were constant outbursts. John needed first of all to minimize his impatience. A crucial second step was to learn ways of communicating his feelings clearly and calmly.

Not all of us are as consumed by this emotion as Pam and John. Most of us have good stretches of time when calm and composure prevail. Yet we can all lose it when the right provocation comes along. To gain control of impatient feelings it would be helpful to explore their nature.

Causes of Impatience

When a person wrestles with impatience, several things are usually happening internally. We will examine some potential reasons for impatience getting out of hand.

Unrealistic Expectations

Stop and think of specific times when you have felt impatient. As you examine each incident you will probably notice a common thread. You will find that your impatient moods were linked to expectations gone awry. Whether your impatience is triggered by a time conflict, a friend who wants to discuss boring subjects, or snarled traffic, you notice that you want one thing but get something else. Your circumstances do not meet your expectations.

People who are prone to impatience are usually unrealistic in what they desire from people or events. They have high standards—which is fine—but their standards set them up for disappointments. Failing to make allowances for the imperfections of the world, impatient people add "must" to their list of requirements.

Case Study

Lou had this problem. He wanted a clean home. He was usually good in doing his share of the household chores, and he expected his wife to fall in line with him. It was intolerable to him when his wife left a few dishes in the sink or let the clothes sit in the dryer longer than they should. Consequently, he found himself nagging his wife to hurry up in her chores and to get better organized. He was not wrong in the things he desired at home; his problem was that he was over-anxious in *having* to get things done. His eagerness to get things into their proper place cost him in terms of his temperament. Lou needed to recognize that there was an imbalance in the expectations he had for his wife. He also needed to increase his ability to tolerate minor lapses.

Self-Absorption

When impatience is a problem, too often there is a deeper problem of self-absorption. The chronically testy person is in a sense communicating, "Do things my way!" There is an intolerance for differing styles or plans.

Case Study

An example from the life of a lawyer, Larry, can illustrate the same point. Not long ago, Larry gave his secretary an important paper to type and was anxious because he wanted everything to be just right. He had tunnel vision regarding this project. Consequently, every few minutes he would step out of his office to see how she was progressing. As she typed he examined the completed pages then looked over her shoulder at the page in the typewriter. As you might guess Larry was very free with his helpful hints. His secretary kept her cool for about an hour of this, but finally she gazed at Larry with an exasperated look and said: "I'll be glad to let you see this when I'm through!" She had nailed him: Larry had been too impatient.

He learned from that episode that he was too absorbed in what he wanted, so much so that he became very insensitive. Both Larry and his secretary laugh about it now, but if he had continued in his own self-absorbed world, he soon would have been short one secretary.

Impatient people are tuned too often to only their own world. There tends to be a lack of sensitivity and empathy for the people with whom they must interrelate. When the focus is on "my needs" a lack of balance develops.

Fear of Being Controlled

Many times, impatience springs from a desire to control. When impatient people are in full command of their circumstances they can usually maintain composure. Impatience erupts when they lose their grip on the controls. These people dislike being managed. This is the state that prompts those sharp responses.

I recall a woman in her mid-thirties who had the problem of losing her composure at work. As Janice described it, her boss was constantly critiquing her performance, and he was very demanding. He would virtually direct her every move. She even had to ask permission to take a five-minute restroom break. Even the most patient person would eventually have problems under such scrutiny, but for Janice, it was particularly bothersome. As a single woman she had great freedom in her personal life and could come and go as she pleased. She had never had to accept a lifestyle governed by tight rules and regulations. At home, she had a set routine she followed methodically. But going from a personally controlled private life to carefully controlled professional one was too much for her. It ignited her impatience.

One of the central desires in all human beings is the freedom to be one's own person. Being created in the image of God, we have the innate desire to exercise free will. Many of us actually prefer some rules to give us guidelines, but no one enjoys being completely locked in by controls, whether at home, at work, or elsewhere. Anxiety builds when our freedom is restricted. Consequently, restriction can easily trigger a quick burst of impatience.

Unacknowledged Anger

Impatience is a close cousin to anger. It is virtually impossible for a person to be impatient without being angry to some degree. As a test you might try to talk an impatient person out of his mood, but be ready for an irritable response. Impatience is an indication of anger that has long been festering beneath the surface.

I once counseled with a man who had a hard time grasping the idea that impatience and anger are companions. So we examined several recent instances when his impatience had got the best of him. Just the night before he had become irritable with his children when they wouldn't go to bed on time. He tried at first to be gentle but eventually he was provoked to the point of shouting. There were other instances when he wasn't quite as emphatic, but it became clear that when he felt impatient, anger usually followed close behind.

Often people who have persistent struggles with impatience find that they do not have a good style of assertive anger. Failing to establish a pattern of assertiveness, they fall prey to aggressive anger. They may cover up their aggressiveness by calling it frustration or irritation, but whatever they call it, it is anger.

Imperative Thinking

Impatient people are often prisoners of an imperative style of thinking. That is, they have very strong notions regarding what should or should not be done. Having powerful, preconceived ideas about how things ought to turn out, emotional turmoil results when matters go contrary to the prescribed way.

For example, a wife may feel that her husband should be sensitive to her emotional needs. An employee may believe that his boss should consider his opinions. A person in traffic may feel that he shouldn't have to waste time sitting bumper to bumper. Each of these "shoulds" may technically be well founded. Yet often correctness is not the primary issue. That is, there are times when "correct" people hold so firmly to their beliefs that their emotional stability is completely lost. Holding too firmly to the "shoulds" (no matter how correct) can undermine one's composure.

Notice what accompanies this imperative style of thinking. The person who clings too tightly to the "shoulds" conveys a lack of acceptance of the person or circumstances that confront him (this is contrary to God's way of unconditional acceptance). For example, one may feel that his friend should be more courteous in social interaction. However, if this individual holds to this opinion to the point of impatience, he is in danger of exhibiting a condemning and critical spirit, and that, too, is discourteous.

This is not to say that a person may not have strong opinions or preferences, but it does mean that an individual is wise to learn the delicate art of knowing when to defer strong opinions in favor of personal composure.

Changing one's emotional patterns is not always easy. Concentration and determination are key ingredients and need to be used over and over. Sometimes it takes years to achieve the desired results. This is what happened to Lisa.

Case Study

Lisa recognized years ago as teenager that she had a problem with impatience. She was the type of girl who wanted to take charge in school and in church activities, and she had a hard time being a follower. Whenever she was not in a leadership position she found herself feeling antsy because she was always able to find fault with others. In her family life she had the same problem. Her younger brother exhibited an array of annoying habits which she felt the need to correct. She spent hours at home in frustration because she could neither correct nor cope with his faults.

During her four years at college, Lisa seemed to gain some control over this impatience. This was due, for the most part, to the fairly conflict-free and enjoyable environment. But a short time later, when she was married, Lisa's impatient nature once again became dominant. Not knowing how mentally to allow for differences, she easily became curt when her husband behaved contrary to her desires. Of course, this only frustrated her husband, and this in turn affected his behavior, which only gave Lisa more reason to be impatient. She was heading for disaster.

Lisa's change began in her late twenties after having a long talk with her mother. Lisa had opened up to her, confiding her disappointments with her marriage and her friendships. Her perceptive mother pointed out that she had seen this problem building for years. She reminded Lisa that her impatience had been a stumbling block in the days when she lived at home.

At first, Lisa didn't want to hear what her mother had told her. Since her tendency was to place blame on other people, it was uncomfortable for her to take the responsibility for changing herself. But the more she thought about it, the more she realized how correct her mother was.

In humility, Lisa determined to make a patient heart her goal. At first it was easy. Each day she looked for kind, unselfish things to do. Her desire was to be less insistent in demanding her own way and more persistently gentle and understanding. But as time wore on, she found that she tended to slip back into her old habit. As she describes it now, her efforts to feel and behave patiently went in spurts. Sometimes she succeeded, sometimes she didn't.

When I came to know Lisa years had passed since that conversation with her mother. She explained that she did have a grip on patience for longer stretches of time, but she had to give herself constant reminders of her goal. She knew that patience would be a challenge for her that would last a lifetime.

Controlling Impatience

Though difficult, it is possible to gain reasonable control over impatience by focusing mentally on some key truths and translating those truths into behavior. You may not become perfect in your attempts to beat impatience, but you can know tremendous victories.

Facing Trials

James tells us, "Consider it all joy, my brethren, when you encounter various trials, knowing that the testing of your faith produces endurance" (1:2–3). How often do we think of trying circumstances as joyful? On the contrary, our common tendency is to view adversity as something to bring headaches. But according to James, we ought to view our trials as opportunities to gain endurance, that is, patience. This seems unnatural. The truth is, it *is* unnatural for a mortal human to sense the opportunity in trials. But when we place our will in the supernatural hands of Jesus Christ, all sorts of possibilities open to us.

There is an old story about the young man who went to his minister to ask him how to develop patience. The pastor asked if he had prayed about this. When the young an answered no, the minister suggested that they do so right then. The pastor began: "Lord, I ask that you bring some difficulties and some very trying circumstances into this young man's life . . ." Quickly, the young man stopped him and asked about his reason for such a strange prayer. The minister replied; "You said you wanted patience and this is the best way to get it!"

Rather than viewing trials as something to avoid, growing Christians will seize upon difficulties and make an effort to use them to advantage. A blind woman once told me: "I don't see my blindness as a handicap, I see it as God's instrument that makes me sensitive to others who are considered unfortunate."

Examine Your Influencing Style

Earlier in the chapter it was mentioned that impatient people are often frustrated in their desires to wield influence. Being led by their inner convictions, such people often behave in a testy manner because one of their firm opinions or preferences is being violated. For example, a young mother is edgy because a neighbor is late picking up her children in the carpool. This woman is upset because she is convinced that promptness is important, and she wants to get this message across to her neighbor. She speaks in sharp impatience to the neighbor. Consequently, though her idea may actually be correct, her style for attempting to be influential is counterproductive.

To overcome impatience, a combination of timely assertiveness and diplomacy are in order. To keep fidgety feelings from festering and growing inside oneself, it is helpful to learn to express and defend your convictions without being antagonistic. For example, if your spouse has forgotten to do that favor you asked, rather than snapping a reprimand you can look for an appropriate time to repeat your request, emphasizing how important it is to you to have this done. A sense of give and take can result, an approach from which all involved can gain. You will feel good because your frustrations are out in the open, and your partner will feel good because a problem has been solved without harsh words. In addition your influence increases.

It is possible sometimes to feel so deeply convinced about certain subjects that we lose the ability to be loving and objective toward those who disagree. When one of these subjects comes up impatience is a guaranteed reaction. It may help to remember that one can have very good and right ideas, and at the same behave very badly in expressing and promoting them. Consequently, dogmatic opinions often work against efforts to maintain composure and peace.

While it is vitally important to have preferences and opinions, it is also important to keep our views in a proper perspective. Because we live in a sinful, and therefore imperfect, world, it is essential to make allowances for contrary opinions and bothersome events even as we strive to improve them. When we accept the fact that our views and preferences will not always be honored, we are more able to handle our relationships. If we make no allowance for differences, our emotional aches and pains only increase and generate harmful stress.

Avoid Seeking Shortcuts

Another trait common to impatient people is their perennial search for quick solutions. They want things to be done correctly, *right now*. I often chuckle at myself when I try to use a shortcut to get quickly through big city traffic. It usually takes longer to weave through these "shortcuts" than it does to stay on the main course, even with the stopping and starting.

Often impatient people are also looking for shortcuts when they begin feeling edgy in personal relationships. Intellectually they know that the best way to overcome their stress is to sit down and try to communicate reasonably, but their impatience makes them curt or snappy. For instance, a father knows that a child learns proper behavior through repetitious teaching. But in a moment of impatience he may try to dispense with repetition and use instead an outburst of emphatic harshness, thereby undermining the overall goal. Such impatience seems very like an emotional yearning for a quick fix.

When we are thinking logically, most of us will admit that few problems can be solved in a jiffy. If we could hold steadily to this thought, we could save ourselves many stressful outbursts and gear down for the longer, more effective road of building influence and establishing rapport.

See Yourself As God's Instrument

As a Christian, you are God's representative to the lost world around you. This is a provocative thought. It makes us realize that what we say and feel is significant, for we realize that many people come to know something about God by observing our words and our behavior. What a premium this places on those traits that are considered Christ-like.

Once an individual acknowledges that he is living his life in service to God, self's desires must diminish in importance. Serving becomes a top priority. "For you were called to freedom, brethren; only do not use your freedom as an opportunity for the flesh, but through love be servants of one another" (Gal. 5:13). While we are free to pursue whatever plans we choose, we are told that the greatest sense of satisfaction comes when we choose to follow the route of living God's love.

In our personal witness for God, our behavior and moods can be far more influential than our pronouncements and dictums. The words of the person who is steady, calm, and composed, are the most powerful. Here is the motivation for working to gain control over the impulses that lead to the over-eagerness that is impatience.

Develop a Broad Perspective

Impatience can be controlled when an individual takes time to examine his broad objectives in a given situation. We have noted that impatient people tend to focus too exclusively on what they believe *should* be happening now. Such a cramped perspective makes it impossible to work at steady development of long-range goals.

Case Study

An executive once told me that he used to become terribly impatient with the weekly meetings he and his colleagues were required to attend with their supervisor. He would work his stomach into knots fretting for the time to pass so he could return to his preferred duties. But in time, he decided he had to control his impatience, and he reminded himself that such meetings were a part of the business world. Even though he never learned to enjoy them, he recognized that they could not be avoided. He found that as he stepped back to examine the big picture he was able to keep his emotions in control.

To gain a broad perspective on matters, it is helpful to ask, What are the attitudes and behaviors that will bring the most benefit in the long run to those involved? A sense of long-term worthwhile progress can help keep short-term feelings in check. If you can make it a mental exercise to determine just how a situation that is currently irritating can aid over the long haul, you can gear yourself emotionally to tolerate the inevitable vexations and even turn some to good use.

Questions for Further Thought

When I feel impatient, what do I do? Am I inwardly edgy? Outwardly explosive?

How realistic are my expectations of others? How do I make allowance for the fact that we are all imperfect?

How do I handle my anger? When do I tend to let frustrations build inside, or am I properly assertive?

In trying circumstances what attitudes do I have? Am I able to view trials as opportunities to gain patience?

How do I keep my opinions and preferences from becoming dogmatic? How can I hold strong opinions and accept those of others at the same time?

8

Infatuation

I sat in the back of the small chapel watching as Mike and Debbie exchanged their marriage vows. I felt a sense of discomfort because I knew that three short months prior, this couple had not even known each other. Now there they were standing in front of the minister and in the presence of family and friends to become man and wife. My fear was that Mike and Debbie had become so enthralled with each other that they were not fully aware of the seriousness of their actions. They were so caught up in the notion of being in love that they hardly had time or inclination to consider the true meaning of the word.

About seven months later I received a late night phone call. It was Debbie's closest friend telling me that Mike had left town without letting anyone know of his whereabouts. Debbie was devastated and sobbing so she could hardly speak. When I talked with her later, Debbie confided that her seven months with Mike had been painful and disillusioning. The two had fought constantly and had achieved little in the way of physical and emotional intimacy. She admitted to me that she had been so wrapped up in her infatuation with Mike that her decision to marry was hasty and without rational basis. Divorce was inevitable.

This wedding of Mike and Debbie occurred over a decade ago. Each lives in different parts of the country now, and each has remarried. Because they had been so thoroughly blinded by their infatuation, they now carry scars. They look back on that time spent together as a dark blot in each of their personal histories. Both can relate to the oft-heard statement, "If I only knew then what I know now."

Infatuation *is an extravagant feeling of longing or desire, often physical, toward another person. It involves a deep attachment or a sensual attraction, accompanied by an unsustainable emotional high. Infatuation usually lacks solid reasoning, being very emotionally grounded instead. It is usually involves male-female relationships*

and tends to have an air of fantasy about it. It often includes a naïve,
temporary feeling of being deeply in love.

The susceptibility to infatuation is definitely a modern-day problem that has reached epidemic proportions. We are encouraged toward infatuation on a daily basis. Consider the appeal of popular novels, billboard advertisements, television and radio commercials, television programs, movies, and popular music, all passing off sudden, shallow emotion as "true love." In these media we usually see an illusion of love that is physically and emotionally intense, but also shallow and self-centered. We are exposed to the I-can't-live-without-you syndrome, and idealized romance is set before us until we subconsciously feel compelled to achieve something of the sort in our own lives. In fact, this picture of sentimentalized "love" can be portrayed so appealingly that we become disillusioned with our solid, everyday love.

Before we go any further, I should point out that not every person who has experienced failure in a love relationship has been a victim of infatuation. After all, there are people who try to achieve maturity in love, but who for various reasons meet a dead end.

There are some personal traits that characterize a person suscepti-ble to feelings of infatuation.

1 A tendency toward emotional highs and lows
2 Over-emphasis on physical attraction and romantic love
3 A tendency to idolize others
4 Overuse of superlatives: super, great, really fantastic, etc.
5 Longing to feel loved
6 A history of sexual frustration
7 An effusive temperament
8 An idealized image of one's parents
9 The desire for a life of glitter and sparkle
10 A sensitive nature
11 Indulgence in rich fantasies
12 Fear of rejection
13 A longing to share deep, intimate secrets
14 An inner competitive nature
15 Frequent mood changes

As the above list indicates, the people most prone to infatuation are individuals with a strong emotional nature. This intensity of emotion plays a large role in their search for the greatest of all emotions, love.

The Four Loves

When we use the word *love*, we can mean many different things. For example, we say that we love our mothers, but we also love an entertainment personality. The love we express for a spouse is different from the love we feel for a neighborhood child. In order to clarify things, let's look at at least four kinds of love that can exist within us.

1. Erotic love

Erotic love gets the greatest attention in our culture. This kind of love involves physical attraction and intense but transitory sentiment. It is a love that feeds on sexual stimulation, and is often the feeling described by the person who has "fallen in love." Despite the romantic excitement, erotic love on its own tends to have a short life-span unless it is accompanied by a more durable love involving the will.

Now, none of this is meant to say that erotic love is wrong. Indeed, it plays a real and exciting role in marriage; it adds the edge of excitement to one's dating life. However, we need to be careful in using this kind of love to gauge the depth of an attachment. Spurred on by sentimentality, it is easy to be swayed by the mood of the moment.

Erotic love usually lies at the heart of infatuation. The emotional high is quite appealing, and in an effort to prolong it and go for the pot of gold that is placed before us, an individual may be fooled into thinking that this love is the ultimate. By placing erotic love at the foundation of relationships, we are heading for an inevitable fall. Erotic love serves best as one part of a larger commitment. It is not steady enough to sustain a long-term, thriving relationship.

2. Love of friends

The love of friends is characterized by warm goodwill and kindly interest. It is the love that enriches the best adult relationships. Unlike erotic love, which is exclusive and private, the love of friends is open and social. The companionship that results can be a welcome experience for a husband and wife since much of their time together must be spent in a mundane matters. Real friendship provides a cohesive ingredient that gives even routine moments zest. This is the love frequently experienced by good friends who enjoy each other's company, and it can be a source of bonding and loyalty for those who share daily work or organizational interests.

Unfortunately, when people are infatuated, they tend to relegate friendship to the back seat because it does not have the thrilling appeal of their erotic love. It seems strange, but I have often heard single people say, "I don't think I could date that person because we're friends." As if there were no place for friendship in romance!

Actually, when men and women pursue friendship first, they are not likely to experience feelings of infatuation. Friendship can actually enhance erotic love and establish it on a lasting foundation. I think of Tom and Susan who tell me that they never experienced much infatuation for each other. They had known each other as good friends for about four years before they ever thought of formal dating. Because of this rich foundation of companionship, the romance that developed was well rooted.

3. Familial love

The love within a family is based on kinship ties, and when it is healthy and strong, generates loyalty toward one another and a warm sense of security and belonging. This love goes deeper than the feeling of friendship in that the bond transcends mutual cordiality. Friendship and companionship have a place in family love, but even when these are diminished for some reason, the sense of security established over time through a long succession of satisfying interpersonal experiences remains.

It is often a desire for such belonging that leads a person into an infatuation. It is only natural for all of us to crave a sense of deep human connection. However, the infatuated person often makes the mistake of trying to seize it through erotic love. Desperately wanting to be attached to someone, infatuated people assume that the way to achieve this kind of love is primarily through romantic attachment with sexual overtones. While infatuation indicates a yearning to belong, it lacks the patience to work for its genuine establishment. Infatuation wants a feeling of belonging *now*.

4. Agape love

Agape love is a deliberate exercise of the will to place Christ-like sacrifice and caring for others in the center of one's relationships. This is the most enduring style of love, and while it involves one's feelings, it is brought into one's life by a choice. This style of love brings the other three to completion. Erotic love, the love of friends, and familial love can all be heightened by putting agape love in action through patience and kindness. Agape love goes steadily on even when one's feelings are not cooperating. Obviously, agape love is the bedrock upon which any mature love relationship should be built.

Wendall had one of those rough days at the office. He was bushed. All he wanted to do was go home and sink into his favorite easy chair in front of the fire. But when he arrived at the back door, he realized that his wife had other plans for him. Having been occupied with their children all day, she was looking for their own companionship to be confirmed. She had many things to tell him, and she was anxious for him to understand her feelings. Wendall could tell that he was important to her. So even though his feelings were not "tuned in" at the moment, Wendall spent some time chatting with his wife. He gave her the hug and kiss he knew she wanted, and he patiently listened to the things she had to say. Wendall's behavior was being directed by his agape love.

Agape love is most needed, but most often lacking, in people who are prone to infatuation. Infatuation involves self-gratification, while agape is concerned about other's needs. Agape love is realistic and able to make allowances for imperfection; infatuation is idealistic and subject to romantic delusion. Agape continues to love whether circumstances are good or bad; infatuation tends to end suddenly whenever things take an unpleasant turn.

Causes of Infatuation

In order to gain mental control over infatuation, one needs to examine some of the factors that cause this emotion.

Emphasis on Romance

It was mentioned earlier that our culture places heavy emphasis on romantic love and sensual experience. We are so saturated with the notion that exciting romance is essential for a full life that we can begin to believe it.

One lady shared with me that she had a deep crush on her family doctor. He was relatively young and very handsome. This woman explained that she had rapid heart beats and flushed cheeks whenever she went to his office. "He's so nice, my heart just melts when he talks to me." (Now remember, this is a mature woman with children; she's no teenager.) I asked her to tell me why she felt that she had developed such a crush. "Well," she said, "My husband is good to me, but he's not romantic enough. I mean, he gives me nice gifts and he helps me with the kids, but he just doesn't light that fire in me the way my doctor can."

This lady had been socially conditioned to think that if she didn't feel a constant "high" with her husband, she was missing something. Having the illusion that romance should *always* be at one's fingertips, she craved it to the point that she began to look for hopeful signs in the other male relationships in her life. In essence, she was subconsciously manufacturing the romantic feelings she felt she *should* have.

In solid, growing marriages romantic love can readily be found, but it is not necessarily the foremost element in their relationship. A survey of couples married fifty years or more indicated that romance had usually been a constant factor in marriage, but more importantly there had been consistent feelings of rapport and understanding that are typical of close friendships. So while it is a definite factor in male-female relations, romance today tends to be highly overrated.

A Possessive Nature

Infatuation tends to be concerned about what can be gained from a relationship. An infatuated person may say the relationship "makes me feel good." Deeply embedded in this emotion is the what's-in-it-for-me attitude.

Carol knew that she had a fondness for Alice's husband, Frank, and she knew that her feelings were on the verge of getting out of hand. Though she felt skeptical of this fondness, she found herself regularly dreaming of how Frank might please her in ways that her husband did not. It seemed that each time feelings toward Frank entered her mind, there were accompanying thoughts of how nice it would feel if she could have a closer relationship with him. In fact, she began to feel jealous that he had married Alice instead of her.

An infatuated person sits ready in the receiver's position. The motivation to love is based on the desire to receive. This helps explain why relationships based on infatuation rarely stand the test of time. So much emphasis is placed on what will be gained that the relationship is not allowed to grow through no-strings-attached exchange.

Escapist Tendencies

Another type of person subject to infatuation is the one who has become so disenchanted with current circumstances that he nurtures an inner desire to escape to something more stimulating. Dissatisfied with reality, the individual pursues elusive dreams.

Virtually all infatuations have a fantasy nature. We all have dreams we would like to have come true. And when we allow ourselves to dwell in this dream world, our emotions soon follow. We could become like the woman who daily allowed her mind to wander in a world where an imaginary knight in shining armor took her away from the humdrum world of a secretary. So enraptured was she with the notion of having a perfect relationship that she spent more and more time concocting perfect scenarios with this perfect companion. Of course, you can imagine that when she came back to the real world of her husband and three children, she felt that "real love" would never come into her life.

Pedestalism

Infatuated people often suffer from what I call pedestalism. They are looking for the perfect person in the perfect circumstance to place on a pedestal. They feel that their own worth would in some way increase, and their life would in some way be enriched if they could have contact with such a person. Of course, this borders on idol-worship.

The person who is subject to pedestalism is subtly engaged in a personal put-down. Such individuals are living with the idea that they are incapable of true contentment unless their dream situation is realized. In a sense, they are subconsciously branding themselves as too weak to gain satisfaction from within themselves. They are placing their hope for satisfaction into the hands of fallible humans rather than into the hands of the perfect God. In this sense, infatuated people are living counter to the biblical directive: "Set your mind on things above, not on the things that are on earth" (Col. 3:2).

Case Study

Sue came to my office suffering with serious bouts of depression. She was having frequent crying spells, and she felt tense more often than not. As she began telling me her history I realized that Sue's problem was one of misguided loves.

Sue said that she grew up in an ideal family. She rarely saw her parents disagree, and she always felt secure with them. In fact, she remembered hoping often as a child that she could have as perfect a life as her parents did. As a teenager she would talk for hours with her girlfriends about "Mr. Right." She could easily work herself into a euphoria by dreaming of that perfect relationship that was bound to come one day.

During high school and college, Sue had three or four serious dating relationships. Each time she began dating a fellow, she would insist on its being a "steady" relationship. With each boy, she was excessively possessive. She loved to spend her dates snuggling and giggling. She would go out of her way to do unexpected favors for her boyfriends. She prided herself in being an ideal girlfriend; extra sweet would be a good description of Sue.

But Sue had a recurring problem during those years. She would become so all-absorbing with each boyfriend that she literally smothered him, and each in turn left in order to get some breathing room. She worked so hard to create the perfect relationship that her efforts backfired. Each time this happened, she would merely look for a new boyfriend and repeat the pattern. She never seemed to learn.

Finally, in her mid-twenties, Sue achieved her goal and got married. She was elated because she had dreamed all her life of marital bliss. For the first few months her marriage seemed great. She would publicly identify her husband as "the most wonderful man you could meet." But even before their first anniversary, it became obvious that big problems were on the horizon. She had not prepared herself to handle the flaws that would be a natural part of marriage. She had such idealistic notions about how a man and wife should relate, that she was devastated when they disagreed or argued. By the end of first year of marriage, she was ready to discard her husband and look for someone else who could more readily meet her expectations.

The fear of embarrassment kept Sue from getting a divorce immediately. She stuck it out for twelve years. She spent those years merely tolerating her husband, having given up her original ideas of wedded bliss. As one might guess, Sue became a prime candidate for extramarital affairs. And in fact, this happened repeatedly. It wasn't long after she quit trying in her marriage that she found herself attracted to other men. In her earlier years, she had always been adamant about sexual purity, but as time wore on, she took a different attitude. "I'm not getting any younger, so I'd better get all the love I deserve."

When Sue made her way to my office, she had been divorced for only a few months. She told me that she hated all men because they were only trying to use her. We discussed her need to reexamine her approach to male-female relationships, but she looked at me with a sense of bitter defeat. "If I can't have it all, why should I lower my sights and just settle for second best."

Sue's problems illustrate how once a person gets caught up in infatuation, it is hard to pull things to a halt. Experience of an intense relationship, even though temporary, caused her to thirst for more. To keep such a problem from getting so out of hand we will examine ways to keep such feelings in proper perspective. This is the process I followed with Sue.

Controlling Infatuation

Susceptibility to infatuation is an indication of the thinking patterns of the individual. So an examination of these thought patterns and attitudes should give guidance to those wanting to control such emotions.

Misplaced Priorities

People who are prone to infatuation usually have placed a human being in a godlike position. That is, they look to a human for a sense of worth, stability, and value. Of course, as long as humans are imperfect no one will be capable of living up to such expectations and demands.

Consequently, to defeat persistent entanglement in infatuation, it is necessary to reevaluate one's priorities. "Which is more important, my desire for God's love or my desire for a human lover?" Such questioning forces us to acknowledge what is most important in our lives. While the secular world fills our minds with the appeal of sentimental, romantic love, we should constantly remind ourselves that we will never be able to experience human love to its fullest until we have an ongoing experience of God's love. Jesus Himself explains this well.

> If you keep my commandments you will abide in my love, just as I have kept My Father's commandments and abide in His love. (John 15:10)

> Beloved, let us love one another, for love is from God, and everyone who loves is born of God and knows God. (1 John 4:7)

The person who is seeking a life of satisfying love patterns can actually achieve that goal by following a lifestyle that reflects God's love. In doing so, the selfish aspects of human love give way to the service and dedication of God's love. When one's love is given first to God, the pressure to have human affirmation and affection decreases. The paradox is that once a person's intense desire for human love decreases, the capacity to enjoy it *increases*.

Case Study

I recall Andrea, with whom I counseled off and on over the course of two or three years. From her teen years her emotions had carried her from one romantic crush to the next. And during the time I counseled her she experienced several romantic highs followed by the inevitable lows. With much persistence, I encouraged her to determine her true first love. While she said she loved God, He always had to take second place to her current boyfriend. Finally, she came to the point of recognizing that her life would be a chronic see-saw if she continued to rely on humans to give her the desired feeling of specialness. It was at that time that she prayed to the Lord, committing herself to give Him first place in her life. When this happened, her need for perpetual romance began to dwindle.

About two years passed before I heard anything more from Andrea. Then one day I received a wedding invitation from her. My curiosity got to me, so I called Andrea and asked her to share some of the details of her engagement. She spoke with a calmness that had not been in her voice in our previous conversations. She told me that she had stayed with her commitment to let God be first in her life, and as a result she had a new approach to love. Her loving had much more of a rational direction, though it continued to be quite satisfying. She found that she was more capable of discerning realistically the strengths and weaknesses in her relationships, and she found herself giving love with little worry about the return. It was a refocusing of priorities that made the difference for her.

The Price of Love

It is certain that any sustained relationship, romantic or otherwise, costs a "fee." That is, sacrifices have to be made at some point to keep the relationship alive. This is true in romance, in friendships, in family life. If a person desires prolonged closeness, there is a price to pay.

It is not unusual to hear an infatuated person say, "I would do anything for her." And at times it seems that indeed the person knows no limits when it comes to doing things for the beloved. I knew one young man who would spend his entire paycheck and give up all his free time in order to impress the woman he loved.

Infatuated people often seem ready and willing to pay the price for love. But there's a catch. In the course of time, infatuation shows its true colors. Inevitably, circumstances illustrate that these people are willing to pay the price for love only *as long as* there is a possibility for a satisfying payoff. I'm reminded of one young lady who fell head over heels in love. After a storybook courtship and engagement, she married this man, vowing all the way that she was willing to do whatever it took to prove her love. Only a few short months into the marriage she began to realize that her husband wasn't going to conform exactly to the standards she had set for him. She became disillusioned, and eventually came to the point of declaring that her love for him was dead. In other words, she had been willing to sacrifice for her true love until she felt that she wasn't getting the proper return. In the long run, her "sacrificial" attitude proved to be artificial.

Being willing to pay the price requires a stick-to-it attitude. There is a determination to give love, even when there is a letdown on the other person's part. This attitude is consistent with God's way of loving. "But God demonstrates His own love toward us, in that while we were yet sinners, Christ died for us" (Rom. 5:8). In our willingness to pay the price we are imitating the love of God.

One's Reasons for Love

We have noted that infatuation tends to seek self-gratification. An infatuated person may superficially seem other-oriented, but there is usually the ulterior motive of wanting to receive. We don't want to go so far as to say that it is selfish and wrong for a person to want to receive love. Certainly not! God has given each of us the desire for love. I would even say that it is the highest emotional striving we know. It is normal to desire to be loved by someone else.

Yet, each of us should ask, "Why do I pursue love?" If our reasons are solely for self-gratification, we will be met time and time again with frustration. Receiving is *a* reason for desiring love, but not the only reason. There are other very basic reasons.

1 Love is commanded by God.
   "This is My commandment, that you love one another, just as I have loved you" (John 15:12).
2 Love is a reflection of God's love in us.
   "Beloved, if God loved us, we ought also to love one another" (1 John 4:11).
3 Love is an expression of friendship.
   "A friend loves at all times" (Prov. 17:17).
4 Love conquers resentment.
   "But I say to you, love your enemies and pray for those who persecute you" (Matt. 5:44).
5 Love provides the most satisfying way to live.
   "And if I have the gift of prophecy, and know all mysteries and all knowledge, and if I have all faith, so as to remove mountains, but do not have love, I am nothing" (1 Cor. 13:2).

Yes, we can pursue love because it can bring rewards. But a far greater reason is that a life of love is what God has prescribed for us. God guarantees that a pattern of unselfish love will be rewarding and stimulating, even when a tangible reward is not immediately received. The person motivated by agape love to fulfill the desires of the Lord, is practically immune from infatuation. Long-lasting, indepth love is almost certain.

Liking Those We Love

A touching scene in the classic movie, *Shenandoah,* is a favorite of mine. An idealistic young man (played by Doug McClure) falls hopelessly in love with the beautiful Southern maiden. In this particular scene, the young hero is preparing to leave to fight in the Civil War, but before going he wishes to seal his love for the young lady by marrying her. So he comes eagerly before the father (played by Jimmy Stewart) and says, "Sir, I would be greatly honored if you would allow me to marry your daughter. I want you to know that I love her very much." The wise father takes his time answering. He strokes his chin with his fingers, looks around the countryside a bit, then slowly says to the anxious suitor, "Yes, son, but do you like her?"

What a pertinent question! Do you like her? When romance develops in a relationship there seems to be so much emphasis on it that *liking* the person hardly comes to mind. While it seems that loving would naturally encompass liking, the infatuated individual does not often consider the fine distinction between the two. While infatuated love involves a self-centered emotional excitement, liking is a more rational decision regarding preferences. While liking still contains emotional overtones, the emotions tend to be more moderate and less self-serving. Liking involves such practical matters as ideas, social habits, and personality traits. I have heard people complain that liking someone just waters down a love relationship, but, in fact, the opposite is true. Coming first to like an individual as a companion and friend can enhance romance.

Questions for Further Thought

When I seek that special love relationship, how much emphasis do I place on excitement and romance? When do I make intense emotion the foundation for my love?

How closely does my style of love reflect the love of God? What strings are attached? How can I love without worrying about the payoff?

When feelings wane, how can I able to love anyway? Can love be summoned by my will when necessary?

When do I fear imperfection in relationships? What can I do to accept the flaws that are a normal part of any human connection? How can I cope with the need to escape to an emotional euphoria?

9

Inferiority

You can't get around it. We will all struggle with feelings of inferiority. Some people are more proficient than others in controlling such feelings, but even the most successful know how inferiority feels.

There was once a man whose experiences in life could well have driven him to feel inferior. At the age of seven he and his family had suffered the humiliation of being evicted from their home and having to look for a new place to live. He was forced at that age to go to work and help pay the family's bills. At age nine, his mother died, and he subsequently spent his youth feeling awkward and shy in personal relationships, particularly with girls. At twenty-three, this man went into business with a friend, but three years later the friend died leaving an enormous debt that took years to repay. At twenty-eight, he asked his long-time girlfriend to marry him, but she refused. He eventually married another woman and suffered a disheartening relationship. To make matters worse, the couple lost their cherished son when he was only four years old.

In his early adult years, this man ran for congressional office twice and was defeated each time. Finally, on his third try he won, but two years later when he ran for reelection he lost again. At another point in time, he was rejected in his bid to become Land Officer. At forty-five, he ran for the U.S. Senate and lost. Then two years later he was defeated in his efforts toward a vice-presidential nomination. At this point, he ran for the Senate and lost again. As you can imagine, this man suffered throughout these years with depression, disillusionment, misunderstandings, and public humiliation. In fact, at one point he suffered from a mental collapse that we might call a nervous breakdown today.

Yet, in the fall of 1860 this man, Abraham Lincoln, was elected sixteenth president of the United States. Though he could have succumbed to a sense of inferiority after a life filled with heartache and defeat, he persisted. While he surely experienced feelings of inferiority at times, he had determined that those feelings held no ultimate power over him. Isn't it remarkable that when modern historians list the greatest men of history, this man is consistently mentioned? In fact, a recent poll of outstanding historians on America listed Abraham Lincoln as our nation's foremost president.

Inferiority is a feeling of self-doubt that can eventually become a dominant state of mind, but it can become dominant only *if we let it*. Our task is not to avoid this feeling, because the truth is we all experience it. Our task is rather to learn how to handle it so that it does not gain a foothold in our emotional system.

Inferiority *is a feeling of personal inadequacy or insecurity. It is usually accompanied by self-doubt and the questioning of one's worth or value. Some people experience and exhibit this emotion so frequently that we say they have an inferiority complex. Others, however, experience this feeling only on a temporary basis.*

Although one might think that feelings of inferiority are easily detected, it is interesting to discover the variety of ways in which this emotion can be displayed. At times the sense of inferiority is quite obvious, other times it is very subtle. As we examine some of the ways feelings of inferiority are displayed, we will note that this feeling is often intricately interwoven with other emotions.

Modes of Expression

1. Feelings of Discouragement

When problems occur and plans do not unfold as one would wish, it is natural for an individual to be discouraged. At such a time one can be particularly vulnerable to feelings of inferiority, apt to feel he or she is inadequate. When plans fail, it is easy to assume that the *individual* is a failure, that there is no distinction between one's performance and one's true, God-given worth.

2. Persistent Worry

The individual who feels inferior allows worry to have too much dominance. Worry implies a sense of incompetence. The person who habitually worries about circumstances is giving a stamp of no confidence, "I can't do it."

3. Arrogance

An arrogant nature is one of the subtle ways that feelings of inferiority are displayed. At first glance you might assume that the arrogant person actually feels superior. But don't be fooled. If a person were truly superior he would not need to flaunt it, would he? The person who regularly puts on airs is actually compensating for inner feelings of inadequacy.

4. A Domineering Nature

Just as an arrogant nature indicates an inner struggle with inferiority, so does a domineering nature. A person who unreasonably attempts to dominate people and circumstances is trying to make certain that his own shortcomings will not be exposed. By taking the offensive, he hopes to divert attention from personal flaws.

5. A Cowering Nature

On the other hand, some people who suffer from feelings of inferiority have concluded that their opinions are of little value. They also assume that the needs of others are more important than their own. Consequently, these people sheepishly keep their thoughts and preferences to themselves, assuming a position of lowliness. It is easy to see that lack of self-worth is a major problem.

6. Ready Anger

The person who resorts to anger too easily is making a statement about his or her deepest feelings of self. Anger can be a positive emotion that involves standing up for one's needs and convictions, but the person who constantly resorts to anger is illustrating an extreme sensitivity to self-worth. By overusing anger the individual is communicating, "I *have to* make sure that things go my way so I can finally feel comfortable with myself."

7. Rigidity

Some people have such firm beliefs that they remain dogmatic and unbending even when it causes interpersonal conflicts. Why do they do this? Usually, these rigid individuals are holding to their opinions because of an inner fear—conscious or subconscious—of being overwhelmed. They assume that the best way to keep from exposing weakness is to hold, even beyond reason, to one's opinions.

8. *Phoniness*

There are times when we all feel the need to present ourselves as something we are not. We survey the prevailing mood and gear our behavior accordingly. This can be an expression of insult toward the self. We are indicating that really we are not okay.

9. *Envy*

When an individual enviously notes that someone else possesses what he desires, it indicates a feeling of inferiority. The covetous individual is not satisfied with himself as he is; there is an unhealthy need for more. Envy indicates the need to have more in order to feel adequate.

10. *Discouragement*

Some people have had such difficult struggles with feelings of inferiority that they respond by giving up completely. Hanging their heads in defeat, these people assume they just don't have what it takes to go on. It seems easier to quit than to persist.

Looking back over these ten ways in which inferiority can manifest itself, we see that this emotion can strike virtually any person. We all have areas of vulnerability, and inferiority can step right into those areas and gain a foothold if we let it.

One major thought about inferiority needs to be grasped. The idea of inferiority is based on the false premise that one human being can be rated as more or less valuable than another according to performance and appearances. This goes counter to the truth that no human being is truly inferior or superior to another. One person may possess superior or inferior skills, but skills neither add to nor detract from the inner worth given to each person by God the Creator. Likewise, one person may maintain higher moral standards than another, and yet even that person should not be considered superior.

We are clearly taught in the Scriptures that God views each and every human as of equal worth. Jesus Christ spoke with the same compassion and candor to each individual who sought Him, whether it was someone who was considered socially superior like Nicodemus, or someone considered a loser and an outcast like the woman at the well. Jesus demonstrated an equal regard for each person and never considered one person higher than another.

When people experience feelings of inferiority or when they try to prove their superiority, it is an indication that they are victims of a man-made game of One-Up, One-Down. Depending on how well they stack up, these people will be susceptible to feelings of either false pride and boastfulness or defeat and shame. In either case, this man-made game contradicts the teachings of Jesus Christ.

Causes of Feelings of Inferiority

How does a person get to the point of feeling inferior? We will examine several factors that can be at the basis of this troubling emotion.

Negative Input

In one sense, our minds are like a computer. The information fed into the mind is stored in one's central data bank, and it is later integrated into one's thought patterns. If a person goes through life having an excessive amount of negative input fed into this computer, the result will be feelings of inferiority and negative attitudes.

A person is most vulnerable to such negative messages during childhood. I have had countless people tell me how as children they were told they would never amount to much or that they were just a nuisance. One woman, Candice, shared that as a girl her mother in fits of anger told her several times that she had been an unwanted child from the beginning. Candice was clearly given the message, "You're a bother to us." You can see how this planted seeds for feelings of inferiority. A troubled man, Kent told me that whenever he performed some task at home he had learned to brace himself for the negative response he would receive from his parents. After mowing the family's yard, for example, his father would point out only the areas where Kent had not been as accurate as he should be. If he scored 95 on a test at school, he was asked why he hadn't scored 100.

We should never underestimate the power of negative input. A person may have the inner strength to fend off moderate amounts of criticism, but he may eventually become weary of fighting it. At that point, the individual usually gives in to feelings of inferiority.

An adult is still vulnerable to the adverse effects of negative input. For example, an employee may come to question his abilities if the supervisor gives predominantly critical communication. Or a spouse may collapse into feelings of inferiority when criticism and cynicism abound at home. We might note that the whole practice of negative input goes counter to the teachings of Scripture, "Encourage one another, and build one another up" (1 Thess. 5:11).

Positive Input

The impact of too much negative input is clear. After all, when we hear frequent criticisms, we begin to believe them. But what about positive input? Can too much positive feedback be given to a person? The answer is yes. It is possible for an individual to receive so much positive input that inferiority can result. Sounds strange, doesn't it! Let me explain.

It is possible to have so much emphasis placed on the positive, upbeat side of life that an adverse pressure occurs. The person who is constantly told how good and wonderful she is can develop a feeling of false guilt and shame whenever her weaknesses surface. It is possible to give such an exaggerated emphasis to one's strengths that eventually the individual feels burdened by the expectations to maintain an illusion of perfection.

I knew a young woman June, who grew up in a home where she says she was virtually worshiped by her parents. Daily they told her how wonderful she was and how she was undoubtedly the finest young lady among her peers. While June enjoyed hearing these words, as she grew older she became more and more uncomfortable with such messages. Her parents emphasized her superiority, but June just wanted to be average like her friends. It eventually got to the point that she felt very uneasy about herself because she had come to assume that she was supposed to be always a notch above the rest. When her flaws surfaced, she felt terribly confused and ashamed.

Positive input is fine, even necessary, as long as it is realistic and doesn't cause a person to compare himself competitively with others. Too much emphasis on the positive can cause feelings of inferiority when the individual does not learn to appraise weaknesses adequately. A balanced emphasis is needed focusing on traits that need improvement and on traits that are positive and commendable.

Underdeveloped Social Skills

We have seen how a sense of inferiority can result when there is a lack of balance in the positive or negative input given to an individual. But another factor may account for feelings of inferiority: not knowing how to interact properly in social situations.

We have all been in situations where we felt lacking in the social graces. Do you remember as a teenager those awkward moments with members of the opposite sex when you didn't exactly know what to say or do? Were there times when you went to a formal affair and felt ill-at-ease about the proper etiquette? Have you ever been standing next to someone at church or other gatherings and didn't exactly know how to keep the flow of pleasant conversation going? No matter how vivacious and outgoing one may be, each of us can experience moments when we feel something is amiss in our social skills.

Because each of us is less than perfect, it is only natural to have moments of social ineptitude. Unfortunately, our culture has placed such heavy emphasis on proper social skills that an individual who feels lacking in this area can develop painful feelings of inferiority. For example, many people feel insecure if they are not bubbly or witty at parties, or they can feel uncomfortable if unable to contribute significantly to intellectual conversations. We often assume that even minor deficiencies in interpersonal relations are a certain indication of inadequacy. We forget that our value as individuals does not hinge on social skills, but on God's love for us.

Case Study

Connie is a prime example of the way perceived social weakness can lead to struggles with inferiority. She had been reared in a home of extroverts. Her parents were very outgoing, and they encouraged her to develop a friendly, accommodating style of relating. In many respects, Connie was successful in her friendships, but strangely enough that was one root of her problem. Connie thought that being a pleasant, outgoing person was *imperative*. So when she found herself in a quiet, introspective mood she assumed that something was wrong with her. Likewise, when she was in unfamiliar social circles, feeling a bit uneasy at being an outsider, she would scold herself for her shortcomings in her social skills. Connie assumed that if she were unable to be vivacious and the life of the party, her worth was actually diminished. She had not allowed for the fact that God makes people with differing personality strengths, some outgoing, some introverted. Connie needed to accept herself in spite of what she thought was a glaring social weakness.

Dominance

Many people develop feelings of inferiority because of being dominated by another individual over a period of time. The dominating person may be a parent, a spouse, a child, or even a minister. In a relationship characterized by dominance, regular reminders are directed to the "inferior" partner that he or she is incapable or irresponsible. Over time the dominated person may begin to question his or her basic value and competence.

Dominance can take a very obvious form, or it may use a very subtle one. Some dominating individuals may be openly imperious and demanding; others may use a quiet and condescending style to be equally manipulative. The key trait of both types is to exude a critical, condemning spirit.

Lynn is a good example. She shared with me that for years she had been hesitant to ever share her thoughts and emotions with her husbnad for fear that he would scorn her or in some way discount her feelings. During this time she experienced tremendous struggles with inferiority.

Another man, Rodney, told me that he grew up with the sweetest mother in the world, yet he, too, suffered from feelings of inferiority because he never felt capable of measuring up to her standards. His mother had a subtle way of making him feel guilty if he erred in the slightest way in his behavior. Consequently, he became highly self-conscious.

Ideally, no human should be dominated by another. One human may be more competent or intelligent than another (as in a parent-child relationship), but it is God's desire that all be treated with the consideration and respect due one made in His image. Whenever one person lives under the dominance of another, the inevitable game of One-Up, One-Down is being played. Unless the subjugated individual learns to mentally detach himself from this situation, feelings of inferiority can take hold.

Case Study

Lou was a well-respected, upwardly mobile businessman who had a problem with hidden feelings of inferiority. To look at him, one would think that he was a confident, self-assured individual, but inside Lou there was a struggle that had plagued him all his life.

Describing his early home life, Lou reported that things were about as close to normal as they could be. His father was a reliable worker and always faithful to provide for his family's needs. He was stern in his discipline, but Lou never thought of him as mean. Lou's mother was a Sunday school teacher and very active at church. She, too, was very steady in fulfilling the proper duties of a mother and wife. Seemingly, Lou and his two sisters had a very average, pleasant childhood. Nothing particularly negative stood out in his mind as he reflected about his original family. Yet when Lou recalls events from his early years, he remembers having feelings of hesitancy and fear whenever he had new or challenging situations presented to him. For example, he hated having to stand in front of his class at school to give oral reports. The thought of being publicly evaluated terrified him. He remembered a couple of times when he pretended to be ill in order to avoid such projects. He also recalls that he felt more than the normal amount of discomfort whenever he was introduced to a group of strangers. Such feelings of discomfort were common for Lou throughout his childhood, but his parents would usually just pass over such feelings as growing pains. As he grew older, his feelings of discomfort continued, and Lou realized that they were more serious than anyone else thought.

Through his early adult years, Lou became an expert at dodging situations that might cause him to experience these dreaded feelings of inferiority. When he and his family went to church, for example, he would rarely linger to chat with acquaintances. He learned to go through the ritual of church activities with minimal involvement and conversation. All the while, he appeared to be friendly enough to those who saw him. No one really knew of the feelings of social inadequacy he felt. If Lou had to attend an office party, he usually made some excuse to go home early. He wasn't up to the small talk at those functions.

One would think that a person with secret feelings of inferiority would thoroughly enjoy a nice compliment when it came along, but that wasn't the case with Lou. While he genuinely wanted to be liked and respected, he was usually skeptical when a word of praise came his way. If his wife told him how good he was in handling the children, Lou would nod and smile, but inwardly he would think, "You probably don't mean it." When his children gave him gifts on Father's Day or at Christmas, Lou felt keenly undeserving. In fact, he was always glad when those special days passed.

Perhaps Lou's feelings of inferiority were manifested most noticeably in his marital communications. An objective observer would note that he was inconsistent in this area. There were times when he felt that his opinions were of so little significance that he merely cowered if he and his wife had a disagreement. However, there were other times when he would exhibit inappropriate and excessive anger, either becoming explosive or brooding. During such moments it seemed that he had actually tired of accepting the position of inferiority and was attempting to establish a kind of authority. As you mght imagine, his wife often felt confused, never knowing exactly how best to handle his mood swings.

Eventually, Lou came to such a point in life that he spent hours of soulsearching, trying to determine the reasons for his struggles with inferiority. Objectively, he could explain to himself that he was as loveable and capable as anyone else. Intellectually he could affirm that God loved him so much that He offered His Son as a sacrifice for his sins. In his mind, Lou knew that he had no real reason to feel inferior.

As Lou was thinking things over one day, it struck him. "I know what the problem is. All these years I've accumulated the facts about God's love for me, but I never really applied those facts to everyday living!" After that he spent hours critically examining his lifestyle. In a sense, Lou stepped back and took a panoramic view of himself. He noticed that every single time the feeling of inferiority crept into him, he was giving priority to man-made performance criteria with no reference to God's undying love for him. He admitted to himself that up until this point, God's love had been little more than a pious-sounding theory.

"It's time that I say 'yea' or 'nay' to God's love. If I believe that God loves me, then I must behave in a manner that reflects it." At age thirty-eight, Lou came to a time of reckoning. "If I really believe in God's love for me, I don't want to make a mockery of it. It's time that I illustrate my belief by committing my mind and my emotions to Him "

In practical terms, this meant that when Lou was tempted to withdraw and demean himself for making mistakes, he would say, "If God loves me in spite of my mistakes, then so will I." In the same way, when he felt uncomfortable in social settings, he took the pressure off by acknowledging that he did not have to measure up to some imaginary standard of personality. When he felt the temptation to act superior, he held back. "If I act superior, then someone else is going to be in the inferior position." He realized that taking God at His word was the key to emotional stability.

Controlling Feelings of Inferiority

God has no desire for any of us to feel inferior. He *has* given us uncomfortable emotions such as guilt and discouragement and loneliness to prompt a return to His loving arms. But He never intends for a person to live defeated by a sense of inadequacy. Like the other emotions discussed in this book, feelings of inferiority can be mentally controlled by fixing on certain unchangeable truths.

God's Unfailing Love

It is true that each human has sufficient reason to conclude that his personal worth and value do not amount to much. When all our efforts are placed in the balance, the human tendency for sin is stronger than our tendency for good. If this were the only consideration, it would be well for one to hang his head and conclude, "I'm inferior."

But there is one truth that can erase this negative conclusion: God had decided to love you and me no matter how low we sink in sin. His loving nature is so powerful that it transcends the grip of sin. And once we decide to invite God's love into our lives, there is nothing that can cause it to go away. "For I am convinced that neither death, nor life, nor angels, nor principalities, nor things present, nor things to come, nor powers, nor height, nor depth, nor any other created thing, shall be able to separate us from the love of God, which is in Jesus Christ our Lord" (Rom. 8:38–39).

Either God's Word is true or it is not. And if it states that God's love is beyond any power, we have the choice to believe it or to reject it. Faith tells us that we can afford to accept God's love as true. And when we believe that as a fact, the natural result will be to live out that belief. Then we will become active partakers in God's love.

"He has granted to us his precious and very great promises, that through them you may . . . become partakers of the divine nature" (2 Pet. 1:4). To be a partaker is to be a partner. That is, we can share in God's love because He offers it to us as if it were our own possession. In spite of the fact that we each have stained our personalities with the ugliness of sin, God chooses to lift us to a level of worth that is undeserved, yet no less real.

When we become partakers in God's love, we automatically sidestep the games of inferiority and superiority played around us. God's objective impartiality becomes our standard. Mankind's subjective, partial judgment is rendered void.

Understanding "Superiority"

If we acknowledge that inferiority has no place in humans, we must, to be consistent, acknowledge that superiority is equally illicit. To put it simply, there is no such thing as a superior person. There are people who have superior skills, who make the ultimate use of the gifts given by God, but superior skills do not give a person superior value.

Most of us have grown up thinking that a person can work himself into a position of superiority. If only we could perform a little better, work a little harder, demonstrate an extra measure of friendliness and leadership, then perhaps we could attain superior status. The problem is that when one person concludes that he or she is superior, an atmosphere is generated in which feelings of inferiority are the natural response.

The apostle James addresses the problem of giving prominence to one person at the expense of another. He clearly indicates that a person who has received a superior social status—wealth, position, reputation—is not to be given preferential treatment over one who is dressed in rags. "But if you show partiality, you are committing sin and are convicted by the law as transgressors" (James 2:9). The teaching is clear: no one has the right to tag himself superior to another. We do not have sufficient insight or knowledge to correctly rate the value of another human being. This is why we are told by God to stay out of the judgment business and leave the judgments for Him to make.

Perspective on Failure

A problem that accompanies a sense of inferiority is the feeling that failure means loss of personal value. If one's true worth hinges on avoiding failure, we are in a heap of trouble! Virtually all of us have more failures than successes to our credit. Even very successful people also experience failure.

Babe Ruth hit 714 home runs, but he also struck out 1,330 times.

R. H. Macy is noted for extablishing the world-famous department store, but he failed seven times before his store finally caught on.

Thomas Edison is credited with inventing the light bulb, but it is estimated that he made 10,000 experiments before he found the right combination.

John Creasey, an English novelist, published 564 books, but he also received 753 rejection slips.

Quite frankly, we would each count ourselves failures if we were merely to balance our positive deeds against our negative ones. Being sin-infested we would each have to humbly conclude that we don't have what it takes to be the "tops." Yet God in His infinite mercy has chosen to lift us to a level of respectability, offering us His love and the dignity that accompanies it. Therefore, our failures need not be construed as proof of inferiority. Rather, they can remind us of the fact that God deems us valuable in spite of ourselves.

Uniqueness

There is only one you. You are unique. God has created no one else with the exact combination of traits and mannerisms. For the rest of your life you can search high and low for an exact replica of yourself, but you will come up empty-handed.

Why? Why did God create only one person just like you? He did this because He wants you to know that you are special! When we fail to acknowledge this special designation given to us by God, we are directly disagreeing with His word. Psalm 8:4–5 speaks to this subject so eloquently: "What is man that thou dost take thought of him? And the son of man that Thou dost care for him? Yet thou hast made him a little lower than God, and dost crown him with glory and majesty."

Crowned with glory and honor! The Bible says that each one of us is given this special prominence. The person who does not acknowledge this will probably struggle with feelings of unworthiness, making occasional, futile attempts to humanly prove his worth.

Case Study

One man, Bart, explained how he had struggled with inferiority feelings all his life. As a boy he felt inadequate in his efforts to please his authority figures: parents, teachers, coaches, and the like. As an adult he worked extra hard to prove that he was the best in his field, but he always felt lacking. One day a close friend shared with Bart the message of God's love. "You're trying to prove your worth on your own efforts, Bart, and look what's happening to you. You're forever being frustrated. But I have news for you. Jesus Christ has paved the way for you. He has already achieved perfection and conquered sin so you won't have to. What you need to do is accept the efforts Jesus Christ has already made on your behalf."

In all honesty, Bart knew that he didn't really have what it took to prove himself. So with that humble recognition, he made the decision to give his life to Christ. By accepting Christ's work on his behalf, Bart came to understand that he no longer had to attempt to work his way out of a position of inferiority. He made it his new task to understand and incorporate the high esteem given to him as a free gift by God.

Questions for Further Thought

What habits and behaviors do I have that indicate struggles with feelings of inferiority? Do I obviously exhibit a sense of inferiority? How do I subtly try to prove my superiority?

What kind of messages have been fed into my mind regarding my self-worth? How can I allow God's message of love to dominate my thinking?

How do I tend to handle failure? Do I see it as proof of my inadequacy? Or does it cause me to focus on God's value of me in spite of my weaknesses?

In my interpersonal relations, when do I speak with people as an equal? Do I often communicate from a one-down or one-up position?

10

Loneliness

A woman once shared with a group of friends the insight she had gained while touring a large furniture factory. As she was being directed through the area where the furniture was carved, the tour guide pointed out a superbly grained sideboard that was still in its natural wood. "Observe the exquisite beauty of this oak. It is the finest timber of its kind. You see, the graining is as intricate and beautiful as this because of the climate in which it grew. These trees grew in a place where there was constant conflict with storms."

Her insight was that humans are like a storm-beaten tree that develops the finest and closest grain. The fact that a tree lived in such trauma made it stronger and more durable as each year went by.

This woman went on to share with her friends that she had often suffered intense feelings of loneliness. As a teenager, she had been a loner who never felt that she fit in with the crowd. She had experienced divorce at twenty-four. Because of this, she spent years feeling she was a failure. She had also had many stressful experiences because she never seemed to feel comfortable in group settings. Yet in retrospect, she realized that her struggles with these feelings of failure and isolation had served to make her a more durable person. Just as the oaks had been strengthened by the storms, she too had grown because of her experience.

People often ask me what the most frequent problem is that I encounter in my counseling office. My answer usually catches them a little off guard. The greatest problem I encounter is one with loneliness. Now, the majority of people I counsel do not come right out and *say* that their deepest problem is with loneliness. They usually come in complaining of long bouts with depression, volatile tempers, marital problems, and the like. But at the root of virtually every counseling situation we eventually uncover a problem of loneliness. Some people disguise it well. Some will not acknowledge its existence, but it is there nonetheless.

Loneliness is one of those emotions that people don't like to admit having. Rather than use the word "lonely," people will speak of feeling misunderstood, or feeling out of fellowship with God, or being on a different wave length. Such phrases don't sound so threatening or hopeless. You see, when people picture a lonely person, they typically think of a misfit or an unattractive loser type. They do not realize that loneliness is at the root of anger, guilt, discouragement, sexual frustration, worry, and more. Still worse, they think of loneliness as a malady that is rarely cured.

It will be helpful to look at how loneliness can effect emotional stability, even in the life of someone who could be considered a winner by most standards.

Case Study

Judy was the wife of a very prominent business executive. She had the look of success in every way. She dressed well. Her appearance was striking. She was a good conversationalist who readily put people at ease. She had two children who were at the top of their classes in school. She had it all. No one would have suspected Judy was having emotional problems.

When Judy first came to my office, she complained that she was in a state of inner torment trying to fit her world into a perfect mold. She felt as if her life were one great juggling act trying to keep her friends and family happy. She worried chronically about the impression she would make in public. Her stomach was constantly in knots as she tried to do all the right things to make her children well balanced. Her husband's schedule was very demanding so she stayed on her toes working to keep him happy. She wanted no one to have any reason to complain about her. Judy suffered from what would be clinically termed a mild obsessive-compulsive disorder. This is, she worried so about her perfectionist ideals that she could not put her mind on anything except her heavy performance standards.

As Judy and I explored why she felt so compelled to be all things to all people, we discovered that the root of her problem was the fear of being rejected. To put it in other terms, she did not want to have any distance in her relationships with friends or family. She was afraid that if she didn't do everything right, she would have no one who would care to share life with her. There at the very base of her problem was the fear of loneliness. She felt that if she didn't give, give, give, she would be emotionally abandoned. Overextending herself was Judy's way of trying to guarantee closeness. She needed to see that her efforts were having the opposite effect.

Case Study

Peter was another example of one who suffered from a fear of loneliness, but his difficulty with this emotion manifested itself in an entirely different manner. He sheepishly told me that he was prone to angry outbursts when his wife or children ignored him or said something uncomplimentary to him. Sometimes his temper was so strong that he said all sorts of things that he regretted later; but he said he simply couldn't control himself.

Like Judy, Peter did not live what people would consider a lonely life. His work as a salesman kept him in contact with many people. He had an active social life, and he was well-respected at his church. So when he and I eventually got around to the subject of loneliness he had a hard time recognizing this as a feeling he struggled with. But as his insight grew, he realized that the times he resorted to bad temper were the ones when he felt misunderstood or isolated from those whose love he craved. He so desired a feeling of deep connection with people that he was highly threatened by any sign indicating distance or separation. His anger was aroused whenever gaps surfaced in his relationships. His temper tantrums were his way of trying to force agreement. He actually wanted to avoid alienation in relationships, but was going about it the wrong way.

Other people have more obvious problems with the feeling of loneliness. Mothers often report an empty feeling caused by spending day after day with minimal adult interaction. Marriage partners experience loneliness when they go to bed in the evening knowing that a rift has opened in their communication. Teenagers feel it when they are not readily accepted by the peer group. Throughout life all people are exposed to loneliness in one form or another. It is to our advantage to recognize it so we can deal with it mentally.

What exactly is loneliness? Is it just a pattern of shyness, or is there more to it than that? **Loneliness** *is a feeling of separation, isolation, or distance in human relations. Loneliness implies emotional pain, an empty feeling, and a yearning to feel understood and accepted by someone.* Although loneliness can be intensified when a person is alone, it is not the same as aloneness. A person can be conversing very effortlessly with someone and yet feel a twinge of loneliness.

Since loneliness is a feeling of isolation, we can all admit to lonely feelings because no one ever experiences perfect unity in relationships. Even the most well-put-together people know the feeling. We all know what it is like to face the gaps that exist in business relationships, in family settings, and even in the closest of friendships. There is no such thing as a person who always feels completely understood and fully satisfied.

We know that "all have sinned and fall short of the glory of God" (Rom. 3:23). This means that no one totally lives up to the potential that God originally gave us as humans. Consequently, no one is immune to feeling let down or disappointed.

Causes of Loneliness

In an earlier book, *Why Be Lonely?*, I mentioned that there are three basic causes of loneliness.

Separation from God

We were all created to have fellowship with God, but because of sin, that fellowship has been broken. Fortunately, God in His love has made provision through Jesus Christ for humans to be restored to fellowship with Him. Yet until we are glorified in heaven, even Christians can feel moments of separation from God.

Separation from Others

Since all humans are imperfect, it follows that there will never be such a thing as the perfect interpersonal relationship, no matter what the popular TV and radio says. This means that for all of us there are times when we desire to be understood or accepted by someone, but we go away frustrated. Some experience this frustration constantly, others only occasionally.

Feeling Displeasure with Self

If we are completely frank with ourselves we will acknowledge that our personalities are not perfect. When we take a total view of ourselves we can find reason for disappointment and even embarrassment. Confronted with one's own flaws, it is easy to come away with a feeling of emptiness and frustration.

Now, I'm aware that as you open your eyes to the broad nature of loneliness you could become discouraged. You may ask: "If loneliness is the most basic of all troubling emotions, can I ever get away from it? Is there a way out?" The answer is a resounding yes; you don't have to be engulfed by this feeling.

Because we are all imperfect, we each will experience moments in our lives when things go wrong. Consequently, each will have times of loneliness. This is simply a fact. However, we need not despair because God has given us a plan whereby we can minimize the problem of being sinful people who live in a sinful world. If we will stick closely to His game-plan (as spelled out in the Scriptures) we can manage our experience with troublesome emotions.

Some people seem to have a knack for bringing excessive problems on themselves. They generate their own loneliness. The following illustration shows how loneliness can be manufactured.

Case Study

Wendy had the problem of digging herself into holes that seemed too deep to climb out of. She was the kind of person who wanted to be best friends with all the people she knew. She would constantly go out of her way to do favors for people in the neighborhood. She was the first to sign up for projects at church or at school. At Christmas time she would busy herself making cute gifts for her children's playmates. Seemingly, she was the ideal mother and the ideal friend.

What people didn't know was that Wendy frequently cried herself to sleep. Although she never gave any hint about problems, she had a difficult marriage. For a while, she took medicine for hypertension. She was under constant stress. Yet, looking at Wendy, you would think that she was one of the happiest persons alive.

I didn't actually come to know of Wendy's problem by listening to her. It was her husband, Robert, who shared his concern about his wife. One day Robert came to me expressing the fear that he was losing his marriage. He said that he and Wendy had been distant from each other for about three years. As he explained it, she was so preoccupied with projects for other people that she had little time to spare for their marriage. When it came time to go to bed at night, Wendy would stay up for a couple of hours longer to catch up with chores. And instead of having some friendly time each evening at the dinner table, it was every-man-for-himself. They had precious little time to grow together or give encouragement to each another.

Robert said that whenever he and Wendy finally did have some moments together, she monopolized the conversation, talking about the things she needed to do. Robert requested repeatedly that Wendy thin out her schedule of activities, but she always responded, "I'd like to but I can't."

Things came to a head one night when Robert heard Wendy crying in bed. When he asked what was the matter, he was met with a machine-gun response. Wendy went into a tirade about how no one liked her or appreciated her. She pointed her finger at her husband telling him how lazy he was and how cruel not to join her in her projects. She went on and on about how she had never worked so hard for so little reward as she had in recent months. Finally, she broke down in long, bitter sobs.

Robert was dumbfounded. First, he was surprised to see the intensity of Wendy's feelings. In this respect, he had been caught off guard. Second, he didn't know what to say. He timidly put his arm around her and expressed his love and his willingness to seek solutions. He was met with a stiff elbow to his midsection. That was when he had decided to call me.

After our initial discussion, I asked to see Wendy. It was two months before she made an appointment. When we met, I saw a picture of depression. She wore no makeup, and she was unkempt. Her face had "I don't care" written all over it. To say that our conversation was strained would be an understatement. When I asked her to share her recent struggles and feelings with me, I was met by a blank stare. Wendy had apparently gone to the bottom of the barrel and saw no hope in sight.

As Wendy finally did begin to share her feelings with me she told of painful disillusionment. She was disgruntled in virtually every aspect of life. She felt isolated from her friends because they never reciprocated her acts of kindness. She didn't like being with her family because they seemed to take her for granted. She felt distant from God because He did not give her the circumstances she felt she deserved. Then to top it all off, she didn't like herself because she was so messed up.

It took several months for Wendy to pull out of this personal slump. Whenever we discussed how she had unintentionally brought herself to such despair, her natural tendency was to place blame on someone else. One of Wendy's hardest tasks that was to bring herself to to point of saying, "I was wrong." When she finally made this admission, she was prepared to take the necessary steps to change behavior and attitude.

There are many people who, like Wendy, suffer self-imposed loneliness. Not all go through the same experience, yet each in his own way actually creates some of the emptiness he wishes so deeply to avoid. While it is a fact that loneliness enters every person's life at times, it is also a fact that we can minimize or maximize it by our actions and attitudes.

Controlling Loneliness

The people I meet with who experience loneliness are not usually as blatant as Wendy in digging their holes to crawl into. And yet, I find that people who have persistent bouts with this emotion usually have a hand in creating their own undesirable circumstances (not always, but usually). To overcome lonely feelings, we must learn that just as there are three ways to experience loneliness: separating oneself from God, from others, and from self; there are three avenues that can minimize it:

1 A right relationship with God through Jesus Christ in our daily walk

2 Loving ties with a variety of others—family, friends, business acquaintances, neighbors

3 Love and appreciation for yourself in the same way that God loves and appreciates you

Some of the following can help you develop a pattern to overcome loneliness.

Response to God's Love

Many people are easily confused about God. They may grasp some of His nature but have a hard time understanding Him fully. This is only natural because it is impossible for the finite mind to comprehend the infinite.

Perhaps the one aspect of God that is most often questioned is His love. Many people wonder how God can despise the sin in our lives while at the same time inviting us into His loving arms. Because no human relationship can match such a love, many tend to assume that God's love will come and go like human love. When they read scripture passages explaining God's forgiveness and acceptance, it seems too good to be true. Some people are aware of God's love, but they selfishly choose to follow their own desires, creating a tremendous gap between self and God.

Whatever a person's mindset may be, it is possible to change one's mental focus and become saturated with the love of God. Notice that though you may not always feel the love of God, it is still there. One's feelings do not determine whether God's love is available. God continues to pour out His love for us in spite of our emotions. "God demonstrates His love toward us, in that while we were yet sinners, Christ died for us" (Rom. 5:8).

When a person responds to the love of God, two things happen: (1) He mentally acknowledges that God cares for him and accepts him, even when that is not fully comprehended. (2) He lives his life according to God's guidance as an indication that God's love dwells in him.

Union with Others

Some people who complain of their loneliness have little reason to feel sorry for themselves. Often they make little effort to join others. Some of these folks may make a few stabs at closing the gaps, but they give up when things do not fall right into place.

I remember one woman bemoaning the fact that all her acquaintances seemed to have turned their back on her. They didn't phone her, they didn't seem to be interested in her. This lady was really discouraged in her feeling of isolation. So, to get something going in her life we devised a plan that would require her to make at least one significant contact with an acquaintance every day. She told me she had tried this before, but with nothing to lose, she tried it again. A couple of weeks later, she eagerly reported to me that she had learned most of her friends were in the same frustrated rut as she. They all desired closer friendships, but each was waiting for someone else to take the initiative.

Think back to the case of Wendy. She was heavily involved with many people, and yet she experienced loneliness. What happened? A closer look will show us that she involved herself in projects, not people. While people were around her, she was not united with them.

Too many people wish and wait for friendships to fall into place. This can lead to loneliness if one does not have friends willing to take the initiative in relationships. In order to stay ahead of loneliness, one needs to be a self-starter in relationships. Don't wait for a friendship to fall into your lap. Seek people out. Put yourself on the line. Don't let your loneliness be self-induced.

Accept Imperfections

When put to the test, we can always find something wrong with the people around us. After all, this is a sinful, imperfect world, and it is easy to find fault. Being critical is something anyone can do, but it also guarantees loneliness.

A woman sat in my office crying because of the loneliness she experienced in her marriage. When I sent word to her husband that I would like to see him, he was eager. Immediately after our introduction he told me of his love for his wife and his desire to build a happy home. But he also shared how he was losing his motivation because she criticized him so heavily. He could do nothing to please her. It was apparent that this young wife needed to learn the art of positive communication if her marriage was to succeed.

To overcome feelings of isolation we must learn to take people for what they are. It is easy to accept someone who is just like you want, but the mark of maturity is accepting people even when they are *not* what you like. I realize that such total accepting is easier said than done. Yet, when you realize that the alternative is a feeling of separation or emptiness, acceptance becomes a choice worth making.

Quiet Time

Recently as I was telling a woman that she needed some quiet time, she began to chuckle. She told me that she would give *anything* to have some quiet time each day away from her husband and four young children, but it seemed impossible. She understood that her lack of time to herself actually contributed to her struggle with loneliness.

At first glance, it might seem strange to recommend a time of solitude for a person who suffers from loneliness. But unless a person has time to spend alone with himself and with God, the time spent with others will be on a what-can-you-do-for-me basis. Every individual needs to realize that emotional security comes, not from imperfect people, but from one's inner relationship with the perfect God. Consequently, as we set aside some time each day to talk with the Lord and to meditate on His Word, we gain the mental strength to face a world full of challenge.

Remember, aloneness is not the same as loneliness. Feeling lonely is an emotion, while being alone is an action. When a person learns to capitalize on those moments when no one is near, then lonely feelings lose their threat. Your quiet moments can be used as an opportunity to share your thoughts and needs with the Lord and to gain practice in being comfortable with yourself.

Sharing Your Thoughts

When do you tend to have your least lonely moments? If you are like most people, you feel best when you are sharing your thoughts, feelings, experiences with someone who is special to you. We are created for relationships, and this means that the most rewarding times are those spent in meaningful interaction.

Many people struggle with loneliness because they keep their feelings and problems bottled up inside. They assume that sharing problems or feelings will not really solve anything, so why bother? One man who used to keep things tucked away inside explained it like this, "After I began telling a friend how I felt about things I sure felt better, even though we never really came to any conclusion. And you know, my friend has seemed to warm up more easily to me ever since."

We are instructed to "bear one another's burdens, and thus fulfil the law of Christ" (Gal. 6:2). By sharing yourself with another, you are living the way God intended; that is, you are setting the stage for love to be exchanged just as Christ did in His ministry.

At this point you may ask; "When I don't have anyone to share my feelings with, what do I do?" Be on the lookout for someone to talk with. Place yourself in group situations where conversations are likely to get started. Have the patience to develop a friendship over time. Don't wait for someone else to be open and vulnerable, seize every opportunity you can.

Questions for Further Thought

How have I created situations that would unintentionally lead me to the feeling of loneliness?

What do I do when I feel misunderstood or in some way separated from others. Do I cave into my feelings, or can I accept them as part of life?

How am I threatened by the fact that gaps are a natural part of human relations? When do I depend too heavily on others to make me feel contented?

What avenues have I left unexplored that would create more favorable conditions for meaningful relations? Am I too quick to give up?

How does lack of trust in God figure into my feelings of loneliness? Am I truly allowing Him to be Lord of my life?

11

Phoniness

Everyone thinks I'm a friendly, easy-going person. People would really be surprised to find out how angry I sometimes feel."

"I don't know what I'm supposed to do. I can't decide whether I should act interested when Jane talks about her kids, or whether I should tell her what I *really* feel!"

"When I'm at work, it doesn't seem natural for me to share my personal beliefs. I almost feel that I'm living a lie because I never let my real self be known."

"At church I put on a good front, but I would be scared to death to let anyone know what I'm like at home."

These are expressions of people who deal with feelings of phoniness. They experience various levels of discomfort because they do not feel free to be themselves. Whether this restriction is imposed by the self or by a controlling environment, the feeling is frustrating, to say the least.

It can be very difficult for a person to overcome the feeling of being phony. **Phoniness** *is a lack of genuiness, a feeling of being fake and not real.* The person who becomes committed to a particular outward image can be entrapped by it to the extent that his inward feelings are inconsistent with that image. One may have such a strong desire to appear agreeable or friendly, for example, that he unwittingly depicts a false image of himself.

Most of us live in two worlds. There is the public world in which we feel compelled to behave in a specific, acceptable manner. This world is often governed by superficial appearance. In the public world, full honesty and disclosure is not always possible; tact and diplomacy usually take precedence over candor. There is also our private world. We all have feelings and preferences that are for the most part hidden from others. In this private world there exist prejudices, dark feelings, personal quirks, and hidden desires. We would like to have more freedom to express this side of ourselves, but fear of rejection sometimes hinders us. (Obviously, there are many times when it is necessary to restrain one's self-disclosure for the sake of common courtesy. However, most of us will admit that we can be far too conscious of our personal image.)

What are the things we tend to do in our public world? Many of us spend tremendous energy trying to demonstrate how together we are. We want to show that we are emotionally stable. We work hard to create an image of success that says "I've made it to the top." We want our behavior to communicate what fine persons we are. We make an effort to look special, to speak with authority, to be involved in important things, and to be super-friendly and likable. However, in this quest to display our success publicly, we are often susceptible to feelings of phoniness. In our inward private worlds, we know of flaws that we dare not publicly expose.

A friend shared with me some uneasy feelings he brought home after attending a family reunion. For three days, he and his wife and kids had listened to cousins and uncles and in-laws rave on and on about all the wonderful things they had experienced in the years since their last gathering. There seemed to be a lively competition among some of the family members to see whose life sounded the rosiest. My friend was uncomfortable because he knew that no one in the family was even near to being perfect, and their affairs were not in flawless condition. Why was there so much effort to put on airs and a false front?

Many things can cause a person to establish a pattern of phoniness, and once one begins to portray himself in a false manner, it is hard to stop. There is often a snowballing effect. The following list includes some familiar behavior traits that can make one feel phony.

1 Saying yes when one wants to say no
2 Working extra hard to create the nice-guy image
3 Never sharing personal problems
4 Hiding one's Christian beliefs
5 Laughing when something is not funny
6 Playing up to the socially elite
7 Keeping one's true feelings locked inside

   8 Remaining silent when there is something important to say or ask

   9 Feigning intelligence and comprehension when there is none

  10 Pretending to be superior

  11 Performing tasks strictly out of obligation

  12 Remaining stoic when one feels like crying

  13 Restraining impulses to loosen up

  14 Feigning interest when one is bored

  15 Talking like an expert when expressing opinions

  16 Forgetting names right after an introduction

The list could go on and on, but it is easy to see how one gets caught in compromising experiences that cause us to appear in a manner inconsistent with what we really are.

Causes of Phoniness

What causes a person to go into a phony act? We will examine several factors that can provide possible explanations.

Fear of Social Evaluation

The phony act is frequently part of the game of social labeling. One often feels the need to create a false impression because of our culture's obsession with judgments. The person knows that whatever he says or does will be evaluated to determine social status. So he does his best to earn good judgments, even if it is necessary to stretch the truth.

The habit of expecting to be judged is deeply engrained. Think back to your earliest memories as a child. When you drew a picture or cleaned up your room or put on your best clothes, what was said to you? You were probably given some kind of judgment, "That's good," "Isn't that nice," or "Keep up the good work." And how about your school days? What was the most important thing to you and your parents? Of course, it was your grades. We can all remember having drawn some sense of value, either positive or negative, from the evaluations given at school. And the pattern continued as you interacted with your peers. Teenagers are apt to be painfully obsessed with peer judgments. It is during the teen years that many experience extreme pressure to conform, to get with the crowd. But this pressure does not end when a person reaches adulthood. In fact, all through life one can be concerned about the way he is perceived. Whether trying to impress the boss or put on a show of religiosity at church, adults certainly aren't immune to the pressure to appear to perform well.

The problem is that an individual can have such a lifelong pattern of playing up to other people in hopes of being judged okay that it can become a total way of life. Some people simply cannot hold up under negative evaluation. They have been taught over the years to live in dread of not making the grade. So they strain to do whatever is necessary to elicit positive judgments. The need for continual positive reinforcement is a strong inducement to phoniness.

Being a Reactor

Many of the people plagued by an inordinate fear of being poorly judged, have their lives further complicated because they have strong emotional reactions to the behavior of others. It is as though they have little antennae that feel out the emotional climate so they can know what behaviors and attitudes are permissible. I heard one lady say, "If the people around me are in a good mood, I'm in a good mood. If they're in a crabby mood, so am I."

It is easy to get caught up in the emotional climate that prevails in various social circles. It is part of our human nature to be interdependent. This means we each depend on one another for support, and we are affected by rejection. It is natural, and in this sense, we are all reactors.

One man, Rod, shared the frustration he felt as a business executive. "I spend my entire day trying to figure out how to please others. When I walk into a room or office I can quickly determine how I should act in order to make the right impression. My problem is that I'm so busy being what everyone else wants me to be, I don't even know who I am anymore!"

While it is natural for everyone to be a reactor sometimes, people who have persistent problems with phoniness find that they overuse this characteristic. These are the people who depend too much on the moods of others to determine their own emotional state. They have exaggerated a natural tendency. They have not sufficiently practiced initiating their own moods from within. Their controls rest in the words and feelings of other people. These individuals are not being true to their real selves.

Discontent with Oneself

The person whose social interaction relies on a phony act, communicates a definite message. "I'm afraid to be who I am. I would probably not be acceptable if my real self were shown." The individual has diagnosed himself as being not okay.

Several years ago, Doug, a man in one of my group therapy sessions, was talking about how phony he felt. He was involved in full-time Christian work, but felt as though he led a double life. As he described it, he could put on a good show of piety with his church friends, but when he was in a secular setting, he was prone to feelings of anger and rudeness. He felt that he fell far short of the correct standards, and as time wore on, he liked himself less and less.

People like Doug have very strong ideas of what they should be, and when they stumble they lose all self-acceptance. They are often perfectionists who continually think about the way they should present themselves. Naturally, this can become a trap. Because these people work so hard to present the right image, they cannot face their personal flaws. They assume their value and worth is seriously diminished whenever a weakness is revealed. Being discontented with their deepest self, they hide under a veil of hypocrisy. But the more hypocritical they act, the more the feelings of unworthiness grow, and they are mired in an endless rut.

Poor Priorities

It is clear that people who suffer with phoniness have blurred vision when it comes to priorities. Rather than having a focus on what it means to live for the approval of God, they are seeking to live for the approval of humans. They sometimes go to great lengths and endless trouble to do whatever it takes to win their acceptance, however tentative. In this sense, they are making little gods out of the people whose approval they seek.

The rich young ruler in the New Testament had this problem. One day he questioned Jesus about how to receive eternal life. In his discussions with Jesus, he revealed that he had lived an upright life; he had done all the outward things expected of a good man. But Jesus knew that his priorities were out of line, and He said, "One thing you still lack; sell all that you possess, and distribute it to the poor, and you shall have treasures in Heaven; and come, follow me" (Luke 18:22). You know what happened. The rich young ruler turned his back on Jesus because he could not let go of the admiration his money bought him.

Our actions outwardly portray our inward priorities. A person driven to phoniness has his priorities backward. These feelings are an indication of the frustration that results from living for the praise of man.

The Consequences of Phoniness

No one can live the life of a phony forever, it eventually catches up with one. The person who finds himself in a rut of phoniness is an easy target for such troublesome emotions as depression, loneliness, and despair.

Case Study

Dorothy came to my office complaining initially of depression. She felt unfulfilled in life. In recent months her life seemed to be crumbling right before her eyes. She was lonely and discouraged and felt disillusioned. But most troublesome of all, she didn't know who she was. To make matters worse, she was angry with herself because she felt that she had no reason to be experiencing such problems. She felt that she should have it all together like the rest of her family presumably did.

Dorothy had grown up in a well-respected home. Her father was a very successful businessman. Her mother was the epitome of social grace. As the youngest of three children she felt that she was pampered a bit more than her older brother and sister had been. Her parents had been willing to do anything within reason to make her happy.

As Dorothy reflected on her early background, she could find no root cause for her depression. She recounted how she always enjoyed herself and her wide circle of friends. At school she had enjoyed the status of being both an honor student and a cheerleader. This meant that she was popular with everyone, teachers and students. She sang in the church choir, and most people knew her on a first-name basis. There had been relatively few flare-ups at home. Her early background seemed storybook perfect.

However, as Dorothy searched deeper into herself, she began to admit that she had been carrying hidden feelings that she never openly shared with anyone. She told me that while her family worked hard to project the image of harmony, she had always had the uncomfortable feeling that the image was false. She also recall times when she felt angry at the shallowness of family communications. She resented having to play the role of a perfect daughter, and she felt cheated because she had not been free to express any opinions that conflicted with those of the rest of the family. Her worst frustration was the feeling that she had married before she had become satisfactorily settled in her adult identity. In short, Dorothy came to realize that her feelings of depression and despair stemmed from a long-standing pattern of living according to the dictates of family and social expectations. Inwardly she had been carrying anger and bitterness, while outwardly she put on the mask of perfection and total confidence.

In our counseling sessions, Dorothy and I went over various strategies that would help her break her pattern of phoniness. Her first step was to develop a communication style that relied on honesty. Initially she had to be honest with herself, admitting that she did have flaws and weaknesses, serious flaws and serious weaknesses. When she came to understand that she need not be threatened by them, she was able to accept her flaws as a part of being human, even as she worked to overcome them. After being honest with herself, she began to to practice forthright communication with her husband, with family members, and with friends and acquaintances. She learned that it is possible to confront without being harsh, to express hurts without being offensive, and to make requests without seeming pushy.

As Dorothy practiced her new communication skills, a whole new world had opened to her. Among friends she became known as one to be counted on because she projected genuine sincerity. She developed a reputation for being real. She also experienced a new richness in her family life because their conversations took on a liveliness never before possible. She learned flexibility in her thinking because she dropped her preconceived notions about how people were supposed to act. She was able to accept others as they were, and she found it freeing.

Although she was in her thirties, Dorothy found that she could do major reconstruction in her lifestyle. She was enthused at the prospect of not having to worry about how she appeared to others. She recognized two major things about herself: (1) she was mentally able to gain control over her emotional expressions, and (2) as she herself changed, she exerted a positive influence on the other people in her life.

Controlling Phoniness

Most of us can relate to some aspects of Dorothy's experience. Most of us have had moments when we wished for more openness and genuiness. We also know how difficult it is to break a mold once we have created a certain image for ourselves. To aid your efforts toward personal growth, let's look at some steps that can be taken to avoid the trap of phoniness.

Our High Calling

As was mentioned earlier, people often fall into a trap of phoniness because they lack a right focus on priorities. Too often, we lose perspective of our highest calling to know God and live for Him. Once a man approached Jesus asking about the highest commandment given to humans. Jesus didn't hesitate. "You shall love the Lord your God with all your heart, and with all your soul, and with all your mind. . . . And the second is like it, you shall love your neighbor as yourself" (Matt. 22:37–39).

Our high calling in life is to know God in such a profound way that He is the central focus in life. No other goal comes anywhere close, and notice what happens when you adopt this goal. You find yourself *less* concerned with the opinions of those around you, and *more* capable of living a genuine life of love.

I recall one dear old man who shared with me how he had found stability in his personal life. He had lived his entire life in the same small farming community, and it had been easy to fall into a rut of phoniness. Although he was known as a godly man, he described himself as having been religious without being spiritual. By this he meant that he had always tried to live a moral "Chrisitian" life but had never focused very intently on the person of God. But as he grew older he began looking into the Bible trying to find the real purpose of life. Specifically, he studied the gospel accounts of Jesus' interactions with common folk like himself. Through his study he came to realize that while he had always acknowledged God's love intellectually, he had never pondered it deeply enough to experience it. In the twilight of his life, this old farmer dedicated himself to study and learn all he could about the love of God. And he then committed himself to live it in such a way that others, too, could know that love too. This commitment, he told me, was the turning point at which he began to experience real fullness in his life.

Ask yourself: "What have I been called to do with my life?" I am not necessarily referring here to your occupation or marital status or to the offices you may hold in the church. What have you dedicated your attitude and behavior to reflect? You will always be vulnerable to phony feelings if you do not have the goal of living in God's love at the top of your list.

Our Perspective on the World

The secular world is obsessed with what it considers success. This would include money, good looks, esteem of peers, a good education, and the like. The main flaw in such a definition of success is that these things imply the superiority of one human over another. Success in the world's terms means that one is scrutinized and measured by other humans. This makes a person very prone to adopt a phony act in trying to impress others.

Wanda had come from very simple beginnings and had risen to the top of the social ladder. Hers was a perfect rags to riches story. In her city she was well known as a connoisseur of the arts. She was familiar with the finest restaurants in town. She rubbed elbows with the elite in the city and state. But Wanda was miserable. In times of honest appraisal, she reflected on how she had left her humble roots and the loving spirit there to pursue the "good" life. She had been obsessed with reaching the top. But to do so, she made worldly desires her life's ambition. She was able to cash in on the world's glamor, but it cost her sense of inner respect.

John tells us that we should "not love the world nor the things in the world. If anyone loves the world the love of the father is not in him" (1 John 2:15). It would be a mistake to interpret this verse so literally that we refrained from any interaction with the non-Christian community. This is neither possible nor desirable. The point is that once an individual is dedicated to living for the Lord, the material and physical pleasures offered by our culture become secondary. While it is fine to enjoy the material gain and social recognition we have earned, these things should be kept in proper perspective. We then become separated from the world in terms of its pleasures and securities. Our anxious concern for social reputation will decrease, and the determination to honestly pursue our true values and goals will increase.

Expressing Our Convictions

Think of some things in your life that you need to go public with. You may need to be more open in your Christian witness, or perhaps you sense the need to be more expressive of your love for family and friends. Maybe you know of some problems that need to be confronted openly at your place of business. Whatever it is that has come to mind, notice that holding in things you believe in strongly tends to make you feel phony. In most cases, you can ease your inner tension by making a commitment to come right out and say what you believe. There is good advice about this in Ephesians. "But speaking the truth in love, we are to grow up in all aspects into Him" (4:15).

Case Study

One woman, Edith, described a personal problem that is all too common. She suffered from the super-mom syndrome. That is, she tried to be all things to her children, even when it meant denying her legitimate needs. She discovered that she had a growing sense of anger because she was afraid to tell her family that she often felt weary in her efforts to please everyone. Outwardly she projected a bubbly enthusiasm in her chores, but inwardly she was disgruntled. She decided to go public with her feelings. She sat down with the entire family one evening and explained that she was feeling frazzled and used. She explained that she needed their cooperation to plan a routine that would allow her more freedom. To Edith's surprise, her entire family accepted her words with virtually no question. They startled her by telling her she was right, and they had privately wondered if she would ever put her foot down.

The actual mechanics of voicing your convictions is simple. You simply make up your mind to speak out and you do it, but it takes a sense of self-confidence to pull it off. The person who states his convictions is expressing a feeling of positive self-worth.

Developing Sincerity

Another important factor to erase feelings of phoniness is the trait of sincerity. The depth of one's interpersonal relations is directly proportionate to his sincerity. Sincerity can be defined as freedom from falseness or deceit. It is an earnestness. People who are sincere are generally recognized as being truthful and trustworthy.

Long ago when Roman sculptors accidently put a crack in a marble or stone statue with a slip of the chisel, some of them would fill the crack with wax. Then later they would try to sell the statue as if it were unmarred. Honest sculptors refused to deceive their customers in this way. So when they finished a work of art they would stamp their statues with the Latin words *sine cera*, meaning "without wax." From these words we derive our modern word, "sincere."

As we mature in our relationships, we will strive to be without wax. We will seek to maintain truth in our words and behavior with others.

Being a Giver

People given to phoniness have hidden motives. They do the things they do because they are worried about whether they will be accepted in relationships. Or they may act phony because they want to receive admiration, rewards, or special treatment. They stand in the taker's position.

Another step in moving away from feeling phony is to concentrate on becoming a giver, and concern yourself with what you will put into relationships. When you concentrate on what you can give you will not have the time to worry about taking. When you become a servant, you will set aside your selfish habits. The opinions and approval of others will diminish in importance.

In becoming a giver you may find that you are setting yourself apart from the crowd; you'll be different. As one lady put it, "I always seem to be the giver; sometimes it seems that I'm working harder to be a friend than my friends are." So be prepared. But keep another thought in mind: there are times when it is preferable to be different. If being a giver requires you to set aside hopes of being like the rest of the crowd, it's well worth the effort.

Cultivating Contentment

The basis for all exercises in phoniness is a lack of contentment. The person who puts on false airs is saying that he is not satisfied to be who he is.

Consistent contentment is an art. The person who wishes to cultivate it will succeed only by depending on the pleasure of living for Christ. This contentment is an internal peace. It may not be accompanied by feelings of high excitement or win public notice, but it is potent. The main benefit is the steadiness it brings the individual about who he is.

Sue Ellen shared with me that she had been caught up in a phoniness pattern of trying to be the great Christian woman who had an answer for all of life's problems. When someone asked how she was, her response was a robust "terrific." Deep inside she knew she was not really terrific for she had struggles just like everyone else. One day a friend suggested that she should let herself be human, and Sue Ellen felt as if a burden had fallen from her shoulders. Her friend didn't expect her to be perfect. Sue Ellen saw that while she had been seeking to be the ideal person, she was making herself a nervous wreck. Once she decided to let herself be a regular person, she found a new pleasure she had never before known.

The apostle Paul wrote, "For I have learned to be content in whatever circumstances I am" (Phil. 4:11). Social status and outward appearances did not effect Paul's inner sense of satisfaction. Like most of us he had had many highs and lows in life, but he had learned to have genuinely good feelings about himself because of God's love for him.

To sum up all these points, if you want to avoid phoniness, practice merely being who you are. In a "Peanuts" comic strip, one of the little girls approaches Charlie Brown, "Yes sir, Charlie Brown, Abraham Lincoln was a great man. Would you like to have been Abraham Lincoln?" Charlie Brown replied slowly, "Well, I don't think so. I'm having a hard enough time being just plain ole Charlie Brown."

This does not mean that there is no room for imitating the kind of behavior exhibited by someone we respect and admire. Patterning oneself after a reputable role-model obviously does not come off as phoniness, rather it can be commendable behavior.

We are fortunate that God expects no one to be anything other than what he is. He expects us to do all we can to make the most of our God-given abilities to live in His will. If we strive to do just that, we will have our hands full. There is no need to add to our efforts by trying to be something or someone else.

Questions for Further Thought

What goals have I set to guide my life? How often do I remind myself of my highest goal of living in God's love?

When I give, do I have any ulterior motives? Can I put myself on the line, even when I know there is nothing to be received?

What about my communication? How am I open with my feelings and beliefs?

Where do I turn for contentment? To people or to God?

What reactions do I have when I know people are evaluating me? How do I pattern my behavior on the judgments of others?

12

Pride

A friend of mine teases people with this question: "Do you think you are a humble person?" If the answer is no the individual is admitting pride, but if the answer is yes he is illustrating his pride. My friend goes on to make the point that humility is a trait that can only be recognized by someone else. Pride is the feeling that causes one to lose this precious trait.

We often think of pride as a positive emotion. After all, there is no harm in a parent's feeling proud of a son or daughter, and it is only natural for an athlete to feel pride after a hard-fought victory. But this is not necessarily pride, but rather a sense of satisfaction or a feeling of accomplishment.

Pride can be linked to one's self-respect, as when a worker takes pride in a job well done. Or an individual may choose to be discrete in what he reveals about himself to preserve his self-respect. In this sense, what we term "pride" is actually a healthy level of self-esteem.

Yet even this kind of pride can be harmful when taken to an extreme. It can create divisions and encourage a false self-esteem. How can one keep pride from getting out of hand? The proper use of self-esteem is a very delicate matter. A sense of balance is needed to keep it from becoming inappropriate.

The tendency to maximize pride is something that we all struggle with at times. In fact, it is frequently at the root of many other of life's struggles. Inordinate **pride** *can be defined as an exaggerated pre-occupation with one's dignity and importance*. It implies an overconcern with one's reputation and with one's own needs or desires. Pride often is exhibited as arrogance or a sense of superiority, but it can also be manifested more subtly in feelings of anxiety or super-sensitivity regarding one's public image. Pride can be experienced in many different ways, depending on the individual.

Case Study

Dan, a middle-aged man, shared with me some of the deep frustration he felt because his college-age son had turned away from him. Dan explained that when his son was young, he pressed him to excel in both sports and academics. "I was hard on him because I thought it would make him more mature." But Dan also said that he rarely sat down informally with the boy just to talk over their thoughts and feelings. He remembered that he did not want to be bothered by such small, incidental matters. When the boy advanced into his teen years, he began to shun his father. He became openly rebellious and irresponsible. He wanted nothing to do with his dad.

As Dan spoke it was evident that he was deeply crushed. He said that he now realized his own pride had led to the collapse of his relationship with his son. In retrospect, he could identify many times when he was so concerned with his own desires that he became a forbidding figure to his son. Too often he had been so wrapped up in his personal needs and interests that he did not communicate a sensitivity to those of his son. Dan determined to be less concerned about himself and more sensitive to the needs of the people he cared about.

Case Study

Kate's problem with pride was quite different. She was single and described herself as prone to fits of tension and anxiety. Her feelings were easily hurt when anyone criticized or even made suggestions to her. She would come close to tears if she felt her supervisor was displeased with her work. She shuddered at the thought of having anyone see her flaws. As her personal insights grew during our counseling sessions, she became aware that the root of her tensions was pride. She was so preoccupied with herself that she was troubled whenever a friend or acquaintance failed to build her up as she desired. Kate needed to realize that it is normal and human to fail sometimes. It was not necessarily an insult or personal affront when one of Kate's weaknesses was identified.

If you think about the times when your own pride has been at work, you will notice that exaggerated pride can easily set off other emotions like anger, disillusionment, defeat, depression, anxiety, and guilt. In every case, there is undue concern with self. Excessive pride reflects a desire to feel important. But the apostle James tells us, "God is opposed to the proud but gives grace to the humble" (4:6). This indicates that we need to examine ourselves to avoid being caught up in destructive self-importance.

Let's look at some signs that usually indicate excessive pride.

1 Tendency to criticize
2 Reluctance to accept criticism

   3 Reluctance to share feelings
   4 Use of a grading system for others
   5 Pleasure in failure of others
   6 Communication style that induces guilt
   7 Impatience with shortcomings of others
   8 Brooding over unpleasant circumstances
   9 Holding grudges and keeping score
10 Questioning God's wisdom
11 Emphatic in expressing opinions
12 Overconcerned with others' perceptions of you
13 Unconcerned with others' perceptions of you
14 Desire to be in control
15 Refusal to admit weakness
16 Importance of material possessions
17 Unpredictable mood swings
18 Easy tears
19 Preoccupation with self
20 Tendency to be demanding

As we have seen, pride is exhibited in a wide variety of ways. We usually think of a proud person as haughty or arrogant, but pride cannot be stereotyped. A loud, pompous manner may indicate excessive pride, but so may a quiet, melancholy one.

Causes of Pride

To understand excessive pride, it will be helpful to take a close look at some of its key elements.

Link to Original Sin

When God created Adam and Eve they were perfect. They were created in the very image of God and were designed to be the crowning glory of His handiwork. As God's most favored creation they were given dominion over all the earth. Truly theirs was a paradisaical existence, but, even so, they came to want more.

We learn in Genesis 2:16-17 that God granted them permission to eat of the fruit of any tree in their garden home with one exception. "But from the tree of the knowledge of good and evil you shall not eat." Of course, this tree is a symbolic reference to the way that mankind was to make decisions. In essence, Adam and Eve had been told by God to "enjoy your beautiful life in whatever way you choose, but leave the decisions regarding what is right and what is wrong to me. Don't try to make up your own laws regarding what you think is good or evil."

This means that when Adam and Eve sinned, they were trying to out-think God. On that day they came to the conclusion that they could live a better life following a way that *they* chose, even though it was contradictory to the knowledge given to them by God. Their decision to second-guess God was prompted by excessive pride. They had become totally preoccupied with themselves. Arrogance and an exaggerated feeling of importance had caused their sin.

The apostle Paul explains how pride can be at the very foundation of a life devoted to sin and defiance of God: "But they became futile in their speculations, and their foolish heart was darkened. Claiming to be wise, they became fools" (Rom. 1:21–22). That is pretty strong language, but it illustrates that exaggerated self-importance can cause chaos in our lives.

But there is a positive side. When we understand pride is linked to the original sin, we can see that our efforts to control inordinate pride will have broad implications. By subduing such feelings of pride we can bring a host of sinful problems under control.

A Competitive Nature

Notice how we are trained all our lives to think in competitive terms. From early childhood, we are encouraged to determine what is better, what is worse, what is excellent, what is mediocre. In some respects, this is fine, since it is necessary for us to discern good from bad.

Yet, when we begin to determine human worth and value through competition, struggles with pride are inevitable. In our culture, we are very ready to compare the worth of individuals on the basis of wit, intelligence, financial standing, talents, popularity, job title. As a result, egotism and pride come easily to those who fare favorably in these areas; bruised pride comes to those on the low end. We are taught to be concerned for our competitive standing with others.

One man explained it this way; "I'd like to let my friends know me better, but there's no way I'm going to subject myself to their judgments. Who knows what they might think of me!" This man was all too aware that if he let his real self be known, he might come out on the losing end, and so pride led him to hold things inside.

Because no one wants to appear to be a loser, we are prone to become deceitful, withdrawn, manipulative, or phony. All these behaviors stem from an overconcern with the grading system that exists among family, friends, and acquaintances.

Assumed Self-Sufficiency

A few years back, one of the news services carried a story about an elderly man and his wife who had died one winter in their own home from starvation, exposure, and pneumonia. At first one might assume that these people had been neglected by family and friends. However, as the story unfolded, several people came forward to tell how they had repeatedly visited the home of this elderly couple offering help and concern. Yet each person had been turned away at the door by the elderly man who stubbornly announced that he needed no help from anyone. It was determined in the end that the actual cause of death was stubborn pride. Many people misuse pride because they think they should have a high level of self-sufficiency. They believe that it is not acceptable to let down one's hair or show weakness.

A lady came to my office whose family problems were a pandora's box. Troubles had dominated her family's activities for years, and they continued unabated. When I asked what kinds of solutions she and her husband had tried, her astounding answer was that they had tried *no* solutions because they had never talked at length about their problems. Each was living under the assumption that their only option was to toughen up and ride out the storm. An admission of problems would have broken their unspoken code of self-sufficiency.

Logic should tell us that no one is completely sufficient in himself. We need each other. Yet excessive pride is mistakenly thought to keep a person from being vulnerable. Rather than take the risk of allowing others to see our weaknesses, we often prefer to take the safe route of hiding behind a veil of false pride.

Struggles with Self-Image

All emotions are a reflection of the individual's self-image. The person who struggles with excessive pride is also struggling with feelings of inferiority and insecurity. On the outside the proud person may *look* secure, but inside there is usually trouble in the self-image.

A person who publicly criticizes other's flaws, for example, is one who is actually wrestling with his own feelings of adequacy. His criticism is an attempt to place himself in a superior position. There is a need to build up the self, even at the expense of a fellow human.

Likewise, a boastful person is often inwardly insecure. Boasting is the person's way of trying to bolster a sagging ego.

A woman once shared with me how her mother had instilled in her the importance of pride, of always holding her head high to show that she was above the problems of common folk. For years this woman let "pride" be her guide. She would associate only with the social elite. She revealed only flattering things about herself. She would consistently refuse to involve herself in any menial tasks. Yet by the time she reached forty this lady felt miserable and was in a chronic state of self-doubt and disillusionment. She had awakened to the realization that her friendships were not real and that even she herself was not real. She knew that she had hidden behind her pride because through the years she had experienced deep insecurity about her real value.

A person who allows pride to dominate is communicating a lack of confidence, assuming that if his true nature were exposed, he would be deemed unworthy. Pride can be a cover-up for such insecurity.

Case Study

Paul shared with me how he broke the spell pride had over him. He was a very friendly, out-going fellow who had experienced a wide range of ups and downs in his life. He had grown up in a broken home and had always been somewhat embarrassed by the fact that he had no father around. As a child, he had been known to make up stories about how his father was working with the government overseas. He was very concerned about his standing among peers, and he was afraid his popularity could decline if it was known that his family life was less than perfect.

During his school days, Paul was very competitive. He made good grades, and he wanted his friends to know it. He was not hesitant in letting others know of his accomplishments, and he developed other ways of getting the word out when he had done well. Paul now admits that it was extremely important to him to know he was better than average.

At home, he had difficulty in getting along with his brothers and sister. He was very concerned with getting his way in virtually all areas. For example, he wanted to have first use of the bathroom sink in the mornings when they were all getting ready for school. He would spend excessive amounts of time primping, making sure his hair looked right and that his clothes were in perfect order. He would snap back in anger if one of his siblings teased him about his appearance.

When Paul reached adulthood, he determined to be the best architect there was. He had good reason to be pleased with his work because he truly was gifted. But he exaggerated this feeling of pride and took a superior attitude. This alienated him from some of his colleagues. Outwardly he would pretend that he really didn't care what others thought of him, but inwardly he struggled with feelings of insecurity. However, since weaknesses were never supposed to be revealed, he continued his facade.

His married life was an up-and-down affair. He was fortunate to have married a woman who loved the Lord and was committed to loving Paul. But his pride caused him to assume a better-than-thou attitude even toward her. When she was having a particularly difficult day with the household chores or with the children, she was very reluctant to seek assistance from Paul, for she knew that he felt he was beyond the menial work of a housewife. His style was to establish himself as the king of the castle whose family looked to him like a chairman of the board.

By his late thirties, Paul had apparently accomplished all that he had set out to do in his life. He was a success in business. His kids were at the top of their classes in school. His wife was a model of social grace and was well respected. But Paul knew that he was missing something. He saw that many people had a dimension of inner peace and contentment that he did not have. He wanted to get it, and he tried the only thing he had never tried to find that inner peace.

He began to study the Bible intensely. He read verses that told him; "If anyone wishes to come after Me, let him deny himself, and take up his cross, and follow Me" (Mark 8:34). And "Set your mind on things above, not the things that are on earth. For you have died and your life is hidden with Christ in God" (Col. 3:2–3).

And he was convicted by 2 Corinthians 5:17. "Therefore if any man is in Christ, he is a new creature; the old things passed away; behold, new things have come."

Through these passages and others like them, Paul slowly came to the realization that if he wanted to have a rich, fulfilled life he had to be willing to set himself aside, and also his personal wants and schemes. To gain life, he must be willing to lose it. This was an extremely difficult concern for one who had always been so keenly concerned to get ahead in life and to create the image he thought would bring public acclaim.

As he struggled with this problem, one word kept coming to mind, "pride." "God is asking me to set aside my pride, he thought. As he focused on that one word, he recognized how his excessive pride had prompted him to shoot for the top in all aspects of life. But he acknowledged that this same pride had gained such a grip that he was almost totally concerned with himself. "Okay, I'll see what it's like to set aside my pride. Let's give it a go."

To make the drastic changes needed in his thoughts and emotions, Paul determined to focus more on others. He had always known the Golden Rule for doing unto others, and he decided finally to put it into practice. He decided deliberately to seek ways to make life easier for his wife. He would set the example for his children by being the first to volunteer himself to serve in household duties. In conversations with friends he resolved to seek ways to build their egos rather than his own. He went on a full-fledged campaign to put others before himself.

"Les," he shared with me, "I can honestly say that I'm a changed man. I genuinely love people in a way I never knew how before. In the past I was so caught up with myself that I was consumed with inordinate pride. Life gained new meaning when I learned to set aside my personal preoccupations."

Because Paul deliberately chose to set aside his pride and its attendant emotions, he was able to let God fill his life in an unimaginable way. He learned that he could control this feeling.

Controlling Pride

When a wild horse is broken and tamed, that horse's spirit is not taken away. Rather, it is throttled and guided in a more positive direction. In like manner, when a person's excessive pride is throttled, the individual is not broken, as some might suggest; rather, that person's emotional energies are given a new direction. That is what happened to Paul, and it can happen to you. Following are some suggestions for gaining control over undue pride, thereby channeling your emotions positively. Remember, the goal is not to get rid of proper self-esteem, but to keep pride in check.

Cultivating Gentleness

Jesus said; "Blessed are the meek for they shall inherit the earth" (Matt. 5:5). Since the word *meek* is not used very much now, "gentle" would be a more modern translation for the idea given in this verse. Gentleness is a trait that has to be developed. It is integrated into one's personality as an exercise of the will.

Gentleness involves kindness, politeness, courtesy, and moderation. A gentle person is not harsh or severe in word or attitude. It is virtually impossible for a person to live a pattern of true gentleness and at the same time have persistent and inappropriate pride. The two are mutually exclusive.

A fine lady named Mable was converted to Christianity. But her husband remained hostile to any religious conversation. He would frequently scold his wife, heaping criticism and sarcasm on her. A friend of Mable's asked, "When your husband is so unfair to you isn't it a blow to your pride? How do you handle it?" Mable's reply reflected how she dealt with her feelings. "When my husband is in a bad mood, I cook his meals better. When he complains, I sweep the floors cleaner. When he speaks rudely, I respond softly." Several months later this same friend learned that Mable's husband had accepted Christ. Mable's decision to set aside her feelings of pride in favor of a gentle nature had made the difference.

A gentle spirit is one of the best possible remedies for the individual trying to control pride. Pride reflects an overconcern with self, while gentleness indicates a primary concern for others. And notice the results; by looking out for the needs of someone else, your own needs are met. Your gentleness gives you an inherent feeling of pleasure. Then too, gentleness is contagious, provoking others to imitate you.

Avoiding Competitive Evaluations

Because pride is by nature competitive, one way to keep it under control is by avoiding the tendency to compare one person's worth with another. Comparisons lead to judgments, and judgments lead either to feelings of superiority or feelings of defeat. Consequently, feelings of swollen pride or of hurt pride can be averted by setting aside any measuring standard that pits one person against another. While measuring external performance may serve to motivate one toward excellence, measuring one's worth can lead to painful emotional conflict.

I once heard of a little lad who rushed excitedly to his mother saying; "Mom, Mom, I'm as tall as a giant!" With a curious look the mother asked, "What makes you say that?" The boy explained; "Well, I made my own ruler and measured myself, and it said I'm ten feet tall!"

Many people follow a similar method, measuring self-worth by some man-made yardstick. Some decide that they measure up well, while others think they measure up poorly. However, Christians are assured that God does not love "favorites" more than "untouchables." He loves us all the same. Paul wrote about this. "For we are not bold to class or compare ourselves with some of those who commend themselves; but when they measure themselves by themselves, and compare themselves with themselves, they are without understanding" (2 Cor. 10:12).

Making Your Will God's

Since pride involves an exaggerated focus on self, another way to defeat it is to focus first on God's will, not one's own desires.

I have heard many people say in frustration, "I don't know what God's will is for me." Sometimes it takes a while for His will to be known in specific areas such as marriage, career choice, or financial decisions. But God is very emphatic in describing what He desires us to do in our overall lifestyles. "And what does the Lord require of you but to do justice, to love kindness, and to walk humbly with your God." (Mic. 6:8).

Think about the transformation that took place in the life of Paul.

How did he do it? What was his secret? We can gain some insight into Paul's formula for success by examining a passage he wrote advising Christians in the highest form of living: "Therefore be imitators of God, as beloved children. And walk in love, as Christ loved us and gave himself for us" (Eph. 5:1–2). He goes on to explain what it means to be an imitator of God (vv. 3–7). An imitator of God needs to refrain from immorality such as greed and coarseness. And we are encouraged to live in a manner that they will reflect God's glory. In a life of unselfish love for others, the self's needs are secondary.

One lady explained her method for making God's will central in her life. In circumstances where a decision has to be made, she asks herself the question, "What would I do if I had Jesus standing next to me?" She said this gives her ample motivation to live according to principles of kindness and meekness. "It's funny, but I hardly have to worry about being too proud when I ask myself this question."

Developing Humility

A friend once shared this insight with me. "I used to think of humility as a negative characteristic. I always thought of this trait as portraying weakness or fear. I once believed that a humble person was someone who just blended into the walls. But now I realize that humility is the only path to true greatness."

Humility is defined as a modest sense of one's own importance. It includes a courteous nature and a deep respect for the dignity of all humans. Clearly, it is the opposite of the exaggerated pride that exhibits an overconcern with one's importance. We know that humility is a desirable trait because it was the most outstanding and remarkable quality exhibited by Jesus Christ.

> Have this attitude in yourselves which was also in Christ Jesus, who although He existed in the form of God, did not regard equality with God a thing to be grasped, but emptied himself, taking the form of a bond-servant, and being made in the likeness of men. And being found in appearance as a man, He humbled Himself by becoming obedient to the point of death, even death on a cross (Phil. 2:5–8).

Remember that inappropriate pride is linked to the original sin when Adam and Eve became enamoured with themselves and tried to place themselves on equal footing with God. Jesus Christ illustrated that to break the grip of sin and its pride, one must be willing to put aside all desire for a lofty position and commit oneself to a servant's life.

Only through humble servitude are we able to achieve the greatness intended for us by God. It is in servitude that we can develop character.

Many years ago, a rider on horseback came across a group of soldiers trying to move a log that had fallen across the road. Their young officer stood by giving orders to heave, but there were too few men for the cumbersome piece. The horseman asked, "Why won't you help your men?" The reply was, "Me? Why, I'm a lieutenant."

The stranger dismounted, took his place with the men, and heaved with them until the piece of timber was removed. Then he mounted his horse and addressed the young officer, "The next time you find a log in the road that needs to be removed, call on me." He then gave his name to the officer; he was General George Washington.

Humility knows no superiority or inferiority. The person who submits to becoming humble recognizes that all people have the very same value before God. Even though there are differences in personal skills and social status, the humble person does not permit these to make a difference. He treats all people as if they were the same. Humility indicates a willingness for servitude.

Accepting God as Love

It is a glorious feeling to know that we are loved by God. And our understanding of this love is a key to controlling pride. There are two possible explanations of God's love for us. Either He loves us because we are intrinsically lovable, or He loves us because He is love.

If we accept the first explanation, as the humanists do, we are in danger of developing conceit and pride. Because we are each stained by sin we must acknowledge that we are not intrinsically lovable, far from it. The second explanation seems nearer to the truth. God loves us, not because of how great we are, but because of how great He is. Love is His very nature. He chooses to love us in spite of our sin. Only the second explanation can lift a person to a healthy self-respect while maintaining a modest perspective of self. To fully acknowledge God's love for us, we will set aside aspirations for self-glorification.

Questions for Further Thought

How do I show pride? When am I openly arrogant? How is my pride expressed subtly?

Am I easily tempted to accept human evaluations? When I try to impress people, is pride at work?

Or have I truly given my self-sufficiency to God? Do I feel I am supposed to handle life's struggles on my own?

Am I a gentle person? Do others feel important when I am with them? Does my life reflect the love of Christ?

How can I demonstrate that I have a care for others? Am I willing to consider all humans as my co-equals?

13

Shyness

From my earliest schoolboy days I was encouraged to capitalize on my outgoing personality. I have never been hesitant in speaking with people in one-on-one situations or in large groups. At school, at home, at the office, at church I have rarely been at a loss for words, but this does not mean that I am immune to occasional bouts with shyness. In spite of my verbal nature, there are times when words leave me and a sense of social uneasiness enters. Even one who seems to have a certain amount of interpersonal effectiveness can suffer from this emotion.

When shyness comes it may only last for a few minutes, or it can continue for hours. It is an unpredictable emotion that needs to be comprehended if it is to be handled. Shyness can have a paralyzing grip on its victims. Some experts estimate that as many as 90 percent of our population experiences this sensation at some time. Individuals vary greatly in the intensity and manifestations of their shyness. Some experience it daily, while others feel it only on isolated occasions, yet it is such a common problem that it needs to be reckoned with.

Shyness *is a feeling of bashfulness or timidity in interpersonal relations. It involves reluctance, even fear, to open oneself up to others or commit to a situation.* The shy person suffers discomfort and a lack of confidence when faced with certain situations. Often shyness involves a reserved and hesitant style of communication, but that can be misleading, for while shyness is usually attributed to introverted people, it is also experienced by naturally outgoing individuals.

It is often assumed that shyness is an inborn trait, but actually, shyness is learned, and there is no conclusive evidence that shyness is inherent. While some people may be endowed with a quiet temperament, this does not mean that they are naturally disposed to shyness. Rather, shyness is a conditioned response to social stimuli based on learned traits such as poorly developed self-confidence and communication skills.

No two people have the same experience with this emotion. Some are so prone to shyness that it shapes their entire disposition. Others experience it only in isolated instances.

Mary was a woman in her early forties who described herself as painfully shy. She avoided groups of people as often as possible because in times past she had suffered painfully from fear and uncertainty in her efforts to be sociable. She genuinely felt that she had little to offer anyone. All her life, Mary had been sheltered from interaction with people. As a child, her mother encouraged her to be a homebody. She had rarely played in groups, preferring to entertain herself or play with one friend at a time. As a young adult, she spent no time getting her own feet planted but went straight from her parents' home into marriage. As it turned out, her husband was very wrapped up in his work, and they had little time to enjoy each other or to establish ties with other couples. When they had children, she repeated her mother's style and kept them close to the nest. For Mary, shyness was an integral part of life.

Stan, on the other hand, was described by most of his friends as Mr. Congeniality. His strength was his ability to put people at ease. He and his equally outgoing wife enjoyed having parties in their home. They would usually be the first to offer their home for an office get-together, and they encouraged their teenaged son to have his friends over whenever he liked. Stan hardly fit the image of a shy person. Yet, in spite of his extroverted nature, he occasionally had real bouts with this emotion. His shyness seemed to surface when he was thrust into unfamiliar situations. For example, he was once required to fill in for his boss at a meeting of executives he had never met, in discomfort he chose to sit to the side and speak only when spoken to. Even then his words came out stiffly. Stan knew that as long as he felt a measure of control or familiarity in his circumstances, he had no problem with shyness, it only enveloped him when he felt out of his element.

Three Forms of Shyness

1. Public Shyness

Public shyness manifests itself in an individual's feeling of awkwardness when faced with a group situation. The person feels inhibited at social gatherings and would not dare to get up in front of a group.

2. Private Shyness

Private shyness characterizes the person who has little trouble performing a task or playing a role in public, but who feels hesitant and awkward in one-to-one relations. Sometimes this indicates a superficial nature in public appearances. I once knew the minister of a large church who could deliver eloquent sermons with ease. But if you met this man privately on a person-to-person basis, his handshake was limp, and he had great difficulty keeping any conversation going.

3. Reserved Character

Some people, possibly as many as 40 percent of the population, are naturally subdued and reflective. Such people are designed by God to be quiet and reserved. Yet many of them view their temperament as a flaw and are apologetic about their nature.

In most cases the shy individual is going through feelings of insecurity and discomfort, and, depending on the person and the situation, these feelings can be excruciatingly intense. As we consider shyness, it may be helpful to take an inward look at your own tendencies and compare them to the following list of characteristics.

1 Highly concerned about social image
2 Avoids eye contact
3 Doubt of one's personal value
4 Tendency to suppress opinions
5 Tendency to be over-agreeable
6 Hesitant about touching
7 Little spirit of adventure
8 Reluctance to appear publicly
9 Slow to smile
10 Avoids social gatherings
11 Easily intimidated
12 Fear of losing control
13 Inward focus
14 Hesitant to establish relationships
15 Frequent sense of loneliness

It is important to note that shyness is not the same as being quiet and pleasantly withdrawn. The most extroverted person enjoys occasional quiet time alone. Genuine shyness is an exaggerated feeling of alienation, accompanied by discomfort and fear.

Causes of Shyness

It has already been noted that shyness is an acquired response, not an inborn trait. It is an outward indication of other inward conflicts. Just as the manifestation of shyness differs from person to person, the causes of shyness differ. We will examine some of these.

Fear of Weakness

When shyness occurs, a feeling of weakness or inadequacy is usually at work, and since no one enjoys being considered weak or inadequate, there is usually an effort to cover-up. This is frequently attempted by maintaining a passive, withdrawn posture. "If they can't see inside of me they won't know that I am weak." Unfortunately, such behavior is often a dead give-away. Even though the shy person may put on a smile and attempt to look unconcerned, the inner insecurity is usually apparent to others.

One woman, Kathryn, shared with me an experience she had at a church social. There were many newcomers at this gathering and very few people she knew well. From the moment she entered the room she felt ill at ease and knew that she could not have a good time. She was afraid of the impression she would make on these new people, for Kathryn believed that she was a poor conversationalist who could not handle religious or social topics. So she decided from the very beginning that she would bide her time and leave at her first convenience. In the meantime she tried to put on a smile and be as inconspicuous as possible. After about an hour, Kathryn quietly worked her way to the back of the room, grabbed her husband's arm, and left virtually unnoticed. She felt a certain sense of victory because she had achieved her goal of looking sweet without getting involved. Yet in the car she was surprised when her husband said, "What were you so afraid of in there? You might as well have been wearing a neon sign that said Fragile, Easily Broken." Kathryn suddenly realized that by retreating into herself, she was displaying the very insecurity she wished to hide.

It is all too common for the person who is painfully aware of his own weakness to assume that weakness means failure and rejection. Because of this, social withdrawal is used as a means of self-defense.

Fear of Confrontation

I knew a woman who was socially skillful with her peers but suffered from shyness whenever an authority figure, a supervisor or church leader, approached her. She shared with me the root of her problem. As a girl she was regularly reprimanded and corrected whenever she tried to converse with her parents. She soon learned that the only way to stay in their good graces was to say little or nothing. If she spoke her mind, it usually brought painful confrontation.

Often a shy person feels the need to play close to the belt to avoid confrontations. To this person, a head-on disagreement is so distasteful that it must be avoided at all costs. He sees nothing constructive in open exchanges of opinions. Confrontations are potential occasions for insults and put-downs, and the shy individual often assumes that in a confrontation he will come out the loser. Consequently, the shy person attempting to avoid potential disagreements will keep opinions and convictions to himself. This often leads to the further problem of re-pressed frustrations in which an attitude of cynicism and criticism can fester unseen. The shy individual may then be unintentionally sending out silent messages of a negative nature, which in turn can lead to the dreaded confrontation.

Bill was in silent disagreement with his cohort Frank, who was conducting a joint business deal in a way he didn't like. But Bill was hesitant to say anything that might cause disagreement, so he some-what reluctantly kept his feelings to himself. In the meantime, how-ever, his demeanor turned sour. He suppressed his pleasant nature when he and Frank were together. Sensing that something was wrong, Frank asked him to say what was on his mind. Bill was unaware of the negative vibrations he was transmitting, so Frank's inquiry caught him off guard. Bill's fear of confrontation actually created additional ten-sion.

Losing Control

People who succumb to feelings of shyness are in a sense prisoners. They have handed the keys to their psychological well-being over to others. In shyness there is no freedom. The shy person's behavior is controlled by his environment; he has chosen, consciously or sub-consciously, to set aside his God-given free will in favor of conformity to someone else's standards.

Ron and Nancy were invited to their new neighbor's house for coffee and cake. Both felt uneasy about going, and Ron in particular was hesitant to accept this invitation because he was particularly uncom-fortable in unfamiliar surroundings. But they went anyway. Once they walked into the neighbor's house, Ron was like a child waiting for someone to show him what to do. He kept his eye on Nancy and imitated her movements. He sat when she sat, rose when she arose. He initiated no conversation on his own, and joined only feebly in the talk going on around him. In his shyness, he had virtually handed over the controls to his behavior and feelings to anyone who would take the initiative.

In shyness there is a distinct loss of initiative. The shy person is quite willing to allow others to take the ball and run. Why? Because the shy person genuinely does not want to take responsibility in the situation. He suffers from relationship laziness, preferring to take the easy road and leave the risks to someone else. Of course, this actually creates conflict. On one hand, there is the relief of not having to work at relating, but on the other hand, the shy person's contentment is at the mercy of other people, and a sense of frustration can easily develop because of imperfections in those others.

Narcissism

Narcissism is an excessive preoccupation with oneself. The person who practices narcissism is characteristically overly concerned with what will bring satisfaction to self. Although shyness may not involve obvious self-absorption, narcissism can be present subtly. This means that a shy person can have such a high degree of inward focus that it is unhealthy. There can be an obsessive quality in one's concern about public appearance.

Claudette had this problem. She often felt shy and inhibited and excessively concerned about her looks and personality. When she mingled with other adults in public, her thoughts were constantly turning to herself. "Does my hair look right? Am I speaking too loudly? Am I too opinionated?" Mentally, she was so concerned with herself that she was an easy target for shyness, but no one would guess by looking at her that she was totally absorbed with herself. Claudette is an example of a person who is not obviously arrogant and yet is narcissistic. The narcissistic-shy person has no real thought for anyone but self.

Lack of Social Skills

One of the more obvious causes for shyness is insufficient social skill. In severe cases of shyness there can be a complete absence of social development, while in the milder cases, there are merely holes or lapses in one's social abilities. The shier a person is, the more likely it is that the individual came from a background of crushing dominance or of extreme social conservatism.

David experienced acute feelings of shyness during his first semester away at college. Unaccustomed to mixing and mingling, he often felt uneasy as he tried to find a niche in his new setting. Reflecting on the reasons for his struggles he came to understand the cause of his feelings. During his teen years he had been encouraged by both teachers and parents to pursue academic and musical talents, but in doing so, he had to place many social engagements on the back burner. Most of his interaction with peers had been intellectual in nature. He had never learned the art of loosening up with his buddies. And to top it off, his closest companion, his father, was also an introverted person. So it was no wonder that when David was eventually thrust out to the world he experienced emotional difficulty.

Studies on shyness have shown that its sufferers usually have not had good training to provide confidence in interpersonal relations. In some extreme cases individuals have been admonished during their early years to keep their words to themselves, to be seen and not heard. This can convey to an individual that he has nothing to offer, nothing to say, to people. In the milder cases, the problem may be too little time spent with parents learning specific social skills. One man told me he had trouble before he got married relating to women because no one had ever sat down with him and shared ideas about male-female relations.

If a person who has never participated in athletics is suddenly expected to perform with the athletically proficient, he will feel out of place, to say the least. In the same sense, a person who has not had a full measure of training in social competence and confidence will be liable to feelings of uncertainty and fear.

Case Study

Ryan was a thirty-year-old single man who had struggled with shyness all his life. By nature he had an easy-going temperament, but he was painfully uncomfortable with his inability to relate in groups of people. One problem was that Ryan could not accept himself as he was. In fact, he often felt like apologizing for what he was.

Ryan had grown up in a small rural community as the second in a family of four. He was often referred to as the maverick of the family, for his siblings got along well with the rest of the family members but he did not have close rapport with anyone. In peer relations, Ryan was not exactly a loner, but neither was he a leader. During his teen years he had quite a bit of fun with his friends, but he always felt more like a hanger-on than anything else. He usually let someone else decide how his time would be spent.

In his mid-twenties Ryan went through several major changes. Both his parents died in this period, leaving no one at the helm to hold the family together. Within a few months time, Ryan decided to pull up stakes and move to a large metropolitan area several hundred miles from his brothers and sisters. He was in for a real jolt. With no family or friends to lean on, Ryan had intense struggles trying to fit into this new environment. Shyness engulfed him.

Fortunately, he was befriended by a man who introduced him to something he had previously been only vaguely aware of, Christianity. Ryan accepted Christ into his life and found a whole new dimension opened to him. For the first time he felt that something could give his life real meaning. Of all the teachings offered in Christianity, he was especially reassured by the thought that he was valuable to God.

But Ryan's shyness still presented a major obstacle. Encouraged by his new friend, Ryan joined a large church that had several programs for single adults. He was enthused about the variety of learning opportunities his new church offered, but he was overwhelmed by the many people he did not know. He felt an inner tug of war. He wanted to become involved in church life because he had such a hunger for God's word, but he was reluctant to put himself on the line because of his shyness. He even considered trying to get close to the Lord on his own without the aid of a church.

As Ryan was sprouting his wings in this new environment with his new-found Christianity, he had one thing working in his favor. His new friend was a stubborn person. "How can you expect to improve yourself if you don't try?" This friend continually reminded him, "You have the choice to just remain shy and uncomfortable, or you can commit yourself to establish a new way of getting along with people." Ryan knew which choice he wanted to make, but he was not sure he could break his lifelong pattern.

But Ryan decided he had nothing to lose and to give it a go. He promised himself that he would attend as many of the church functions for singles as his schedule would permit. In fact, he volunteered to serve on a committee or two to be assured of regular involvement. Each time he was with people, he made a real effort not to be just a passive observer in the conversation; he actually sought opportunities to initiate discussions. Another goal was to let others know that he was interested in them. Ryan realized that his shyness had caused him to be too self-absorbed.

Ryan's efforts did not produce changes overnight, but changes did come— gradually. Even after a couple of years in his efforts to be more outgoing he still found it was work. His old feelings of shyness seemed natural to him, and an outgoing nature seemed foreign. Yet he persisted. He constantly reminded himself that extreme shyness was a choice. He could decide either to allow his feelings of social discomfort to dominate, or he could plow ahead and work to have a more satisfactory lifestyle of openness and involvement. Realizing that he could choose to be the initiator in relationships prompted Ryan to be more and more consistent in breaking his lifelong pattern of shyness.

Controlling Shyness

In seeking solutions to painful shyness, one should remember that a personality overhaul is not in order. A quiet, unassertive personality has many appealing features. No one type of personality style is better than another. Shyness occurs when a person is seeking to control feelings of hesitancy and discomfort. These feelings of shyness can be controlled within each different personality. With this in mind, let's explore several key steps in gaining mental control over this emotion.

Accepting Self

Often shyness occurs because the individual has no sense of self-acceptance. This lack of self-acceptance can grow to a level that intensifies the original shyness. It becomes a never-ending cycle.

Our American culture tends to put such a high premium on the vivacious, outgoing personality that we are subconsciously programmed to believe that anything short of this is second-rate. In any social setting who tend to be the most magnetic people? Usually we will find that most attention is given to the bubbly, extroverted people. The quiet, unassuming types too often fill in the background, and we interpret this to mean it is better to be sociable and verbal.

Anyone who subscribes to the idea of a hierarchy of personality styles will have feelings of self-doubt at some time, for such a one's self-acceptance is only conditional. Yet we know that all people, no matter what their background or personalities, are equally acceptable to God for "God is not one to show partiality" (Acts 10:34).

In practical terms this means that there be no distinctions of the worth of an individual based on arbitrary human standards. If a person is witty, he is acceptable. If a person is bland, he also is acceptable. Whether a person adds great depth to conversation or has very little to say, his ultimate acceptance is assured. Consequently, an individual who has a hard time fitting into a social climate may conclude that he needs to make personal improvements, but that does not detract one iota from his God-given personal value.

The first step toward overcoming the discomfort of shyness is to take yourself for what you are. You may decide to work to change certain traits or habits, but it is vitally important that you maintain an unchanging sense of self-value. If God says He has given His love to all in equal portions, who are we to disagree?

Taking Risks

One day as I was standing in the lobby of my church a man in his early twenties walked up to me, hesitantly introduced himself, said a few words, then left. Not far behind, came one of the man's friends. "You probably didn't know it," he said, "but that guy you just talked to was fulfilling an assignment. He has always been real shy, so he promised that he would initiate conversation with three stangers per day."

As I thought about this man's effort to be more gregarious, I felt that he would probably succeed in his task. He was willing to stick his neck out and take a risk.

Change is often risky. And when one attempts to change from being socially shy to being socially confident, there is an element of uncertainty. In any interaction between humans, the outcome is uncertain. A skilled conversationalist knows how to be flexible, and to go with the flow of a discussion. A shy person can be threatened by the unknown, but flexibility can be learned.

Despite the fact that shyness is often an expression of the need to be in control, the shy person often forfeits the social controls to others rather than take a risk. But if shyness is to be tamed, there will be an allowance for freedom. Cultivate openness that does not need to stay only with the familiar, one that can recognize and enjoy the free-floating nature of relationships.

One young woman, Teri, put herself to the test of being a risk-taker to overcome her shyness. She had been recently divorced and was trying to establish a whole new way of life. She knew that her shyness had previously led her to make the "safe" decision to marry her hometown boyfriend, even when she knew it was not a good decision. So now, in her effort to become more open, Teri decided to join several groups, both at work and at church. As she was trying to make new friends, she determined to be honest in letting them know the real Teri. She even initiated phone calls to invite friends to drop by her apartment. While these actions may have seemed commonplace to some, they represented a huge risk to Teri. But she was determined that her shyness was not going to cause her to settle for second best in the future.

Relying on God

A person susceptible to shyness is clearly aware of his own weaknesses. He knows that he is capable of making mistakes, blunders, and bad impressions. In addition, there is an underlying fear that the humiliation of not measuring up to the prevailing social standard would be too much to bear.

If we were left to rely on our own strength for social confidence, we would all suffer insecurity. After all, as sinners we are imperfect. However, a person who has committed himself to the Lord has an extra power-pack to draw from. We are not left to live life merely on our own strength; rather, we have the assurance of knowing that God will provide the necessities to make life satisfactory. "For God has not given us a spirit of timidity, but of power and love and discipline" (2 Tim. 1:7).

Christians need not fall back on the words, "I can't" (actually it would be more accurate to say, "I won't"). Empowered by the inner strength and discipline supplied by God Himself, the believer can set his mind to overcome the fear at the basis of shyness. This doesn't mean, as we have said, that a person must completely rearrange his personality, but it does mean that an individual can deliberately focus on being more other-oriented in social settings. If we look more intently to God than to humans for our sense of inner stability, we are less concerned with potential failure and more focused on probable successes.

When I was in my graduate training I felt a distinct shyness when I was among professors and upper-level graduate students. In conversations, I felt I should either say something intelligent or say nothing at all— I remained silent quite a bit. But one of my friends said to me, "Wake up, Les. You don't have to worry about what all these brainy people think about you. Besides, I thought you were supposed to worship God, not professors!" My friend had hit me right between the eyes. He brought home the message of 2 Timothy 1:7. God never did intend for me to be timid. It was up to me then to claim His power.

An Outward Focus

As we have noted, shyness can cause an unhealthy focus on personal desires or traits. A natural way to break this habit is to give one's mental and emotional attention to others. In practical terms this involves a deliberate effort to accertain the feelings and experiences of others, to understand the world from the other person's point of reference.

Eugene was convinced that he was too self-conscious. He spent far too much time worrying about whether he was going to say the right or wrong thing, and he wanted to overcome this tendency. He spent an entire week engaging in conversations during which he would focus on his companion. His intention was to set aside his own feelings and openly demonstrate that he was interested in the feelings and reactions of others. For example, if a man expressed frustration at work about meeting a deadline, Eugene would say, "That must make you feel hurried. What do you do when time gets down to the wire?" Or when he went home and his wife wanted to tell him about her phone conversation with Aunt Sue he would say, "It sounds like you had a lot of catching up to do. Tell me more." After doing this for one week (a week is a long time for this experiment), Eugene was genuinely excited. "For the first time I've really proved that I can get away from my inner concerns and have a real interest in people. And, boy, does it make a difference!"

Most of us will find that we live in a world of people who are yearning to be heard and understood. Our world needs confident, interested people willing to set aside their own inner worries and concentrate on making others feel noticed. When this is attempted shyness can be replaced by a caring, communicative nature.

Questions for Further Thought

When do I tend to be most vulnerable to feelings of shyness? Do I look to people for their approval so I can feel good about myself?

What am I afraid of in social interactions? Am I fearful of showing my inadequacies? Am I afraid of disapproval?

How much structure do I need in interrelations? Can I allow for a free-floating atmosphere?

Do I focus too intently on my personal strengths and weaknesses? Do I have as my first goal showing an interest toward others?

Have I drawn upon the power given to me by God? Have I made Him my ultimate source of security?

14

Worry

We are living in uneasy times. Ours is an uptight, stressed-out world. We can constantly find things to worry about. Think about it. We worry about time. We worry about money. We worry about family relations, the boss, our weekend plans, the weather, our children. You might say that we are a society of worraholics!

Exactly what is worry anyway? As I researched this subject, I was amused to learn that our word *worry* comes from an Anglo-Saxon root meaning "to strangle or give pain." *This implies that* **worry** *is a choking, harmful emotion that can sap one's energy and strength.* **Worry** *is a feeling of uneasiness, apprehension, and distress, usually about something impending or anticipated in the future.* Actually, worry is often a mixture of fear and anger. That is, in worry there is both a feeling of timidity and a sense of irritation.

Worriers come in all forms; there is no typical worrier. While we often think of worriers as fidgety, hysterical people, worry can be imbedded deep in the quiet, subdued personality, and even in strong, powerful personalities. We are all susceptible to this emotion. In order to examine one's tendency toward worry, I have listed some indicators that signify inner struggles with this emotion.

1 Tendency to dwell on problems
2 Upset by small annoyances
3 Insecurity about the future
4 Inflation of minor problems
5 Feeling out of touch with God
6 Sour attitude about interpersonal conflict
7 Naturally critical
8 Physical symptoms, such as headache, backache, nervous stomach, grinding teeth

 9 Significant problems in communication
10 Hard to accept defeats
11 Burn-out feeling
12 Loose ends hard to handle
13 Usually under strain
14 Many phobias
15 Time conscious
16 Doubts about ability to perform
17 Easily frustrated
18 Rehash of past events
19 Defensive in confrontations

Looking over this list of traits that can accompany worry, we can see that it is a broadly based emotion. It is universal, and yet the individual who fails to master this emotion is likely to lose his enjoyment of life. Since we are told in the Scriptures to be anxious for nothing, it is to our advantage to understand the nature of worry so we can gain victory over it.

Causes of Worry

Since worry is an emotion that is displayed in a multifaceted manner, we can expect to find that it is caused by varying factors. We will examine some ways in which worry can develop in an otherwise normal person.

Overemphasis on Responsibilities

At first glance it might seem strange that a Christian therapist would say that individuals can actually be *too* responsible in their attitudes. In fact, you might expect me to say the opposite: "Be more responsible and your worries will cease!"

But the truth is that some people feel so compelled to have their lives perfectly organized that they generate worry and tension. These people assume that everything in their lives should be in tip-top order before they can be content. When I counsel with these people I find that their sense of responsibility is often so exaggerated that a guilt-laden sense of duty is injected into most aspects of their lives. This intense feeling of obligation often creates recurring anxieties. Their right sense of responsibility can lead to harmful patterns of emotional expression.

Have you ever observed perennial worriers? They exhaust them-selves and everyone around them in their efforts to carefully enact their duties. For example, when a chronic worrier has guests, there are hectic preparations beforehand and insistent demands that absolutely, positively those guests must see nothing out of proper place. Great energy is poured out to get the house cleaned, but at what cost? The worrier's stomach is tied up in knots, and the entire family is driven to utter frustration! Meeting responsibilities takes priority over all else, including enjoying the guests. Or how about the super-responsible employee? On the job this person concentrates so keenly on getting things done properly that no allowance is made for occasional interper-sonal exchanges. Responsibilities are taken care of, but no friendships are developed. What a shame!

Worriers tend to expend enormous amounts of energy trying to do things right, but there is often such a rigid mindset that there is little tolerance of the flaws in the people and situations around them. Such people are not wrong to take their responsibilities seriously, but they need to keep things in balance. When a person insists on having things perfect at all costs, the ability to relax in our unpredictable world is lost.

Unrealistic Ideals

Worriers tend to be idealists. You might not think so when you hear a worrier complain about all that has gone wrong or the problems that lie ahead. Their communication can sound very negative. But behind this fretting are idealistic assumptions about how things *ought* to be. Worriers cling tenaciously to their ought's and never face the impos-sibility of their expectations.

To be honest, we all know that not many things will work out exactly the way they ought to. The one who clings stubbornly to idealistic expectations is asking for trouble. I have yet to meet the family who enjoys consistently perfect and sympathetic communication. Nor have I heard of a business or a club or a congregation that is completely free of problems. Yet I counsel with many people who have driven them-selves to distraction by holding unrealistically to preconceived notions of how things ought to be.

Case Study

One woman in particular comes to my mind—Trudy. She was a person who publicly presented the picture of complete composure. All of her life she had been drilled to speak and act properly, and to a great extent she had complied with those teachings. That was in her public life. Her private world was an entirely different matter. Behind the walls of her own home, Trudy was an emotional wreck. She rarely had a peaceful day. Before her marriage and the start of her family, she had a mental image of how perfect her family life would be. But once into that family life, she found things entirely different. She would become tense if one of her children misbehaved or displeased her in some way. The children, of course, could sense her tension, and they in turn felt tight. When her husband did not speak or act in the "prescribed" way, Trudy would worry about the state of their marriage. This tendency to worry and fret about her family life was so demoralizing that her children were afraid of her and her husband tried to avoid her whenever possible. Trudy's idealism was her greatest enemy. It was only when she became more realistic in her expectations and relationships with family and friends that she was able to get a grip on her worries.

It is certainly helpful for each person to have ideals and try to fulfill them. Jesus Christ Himself encourages us to be perfect (Matt. 5:48). Yet, there is such a thing as overdoing a good thing. The person who clings to idealistic notions to the exclusion of everything else is not grasping the whole of God's truth. Scripture tells us that we are all sinful and fall short of God's glory (Rom. 5:12). So when no allowance is made for the stains in life brought about by sin, worry is guaranteed.

Excessive Fear

I knew a man who lived in perpetual fear. It seemed as though he was tormented by one fear after another. At work he feared the displeasure of his supervisor. At home he feared that he would not discipline the children properly or would not please his wife. At church and among neighbors he was afraid of creating wrong impressions. While each concern was legitimate, he was so overwrought that he was in constant nervous turmoil.

We are all afraid of something, and this is nothing to be ashamed of since we are fallible humans. When one is face to face with a trying situation, fear can be a normal response. But we humans are puzzling creatures. Despite God's assurance that He will provide us with the strength we need, we let fear have total control. Fear can grip us in many situations.

We worry about having a babysitter; something might happen to the children.

We worry about money problems, as if worry will somehow solve them.

We are afraid of a breakdown in communication, worrying that interpersonal problems can be too hard to solve.

We worry about our personal weaknesses, fearing that they are a
sign of an immature or unstable personality.

There is no need for fear to be given the full attention it receives in
such instances. Yet because of the powerful desire to completely rid life
of its pains, we fear everything that might cause discomfort or disorder.
The irony is that fear itself brings the very pain we wish to avoid.

The person who tries to achieve emotional stability and security
through fear is exercising a kind of faith in reverse. That person is
communicating, "I have faith that things won't work out." Of course,
you can see that this sabotages the contentment offered us by God.
While we have good reason to be apprehensive about some problems
that confront us, we can hold even more firmly to the fact that our God
is able and willing to supply all our needs in any circumstance (Phil.
4:19). The person who chooses persistent worry and fear as his solution
is ignoring this truth.

A Fragile Ego

Excessive worry is a sure indication that the individual feels fragile
at the core. The worrier assumes that he is incompetent. The individual
feels that he is helpless and powerless to cope with problems. Worry
also implies an excessive need to be protected from stress. In a sense, a
person who worries is crying out, "Save me!"

How does a fragile ego that is so often the foundation of worry
develop? In most cases, childhood experiences play a strong role in
determining how an individual learns to grapple with tensions. Several
childhood patterns can hinder a person's later abilities in problem-
solving.

1. *The rigid control pattern.* Some individuals grow up in an environment where orders and commands are the normal way of handling
problems. These people are always sternly told what to do, and defiance of authority is not permitted. As you might guess, the person
who develops in such an atmosphere worries constantly for fear of
doing wrong. As adults, these people continue to fear other conflicts.

2. *The soft, dependent pattern.* Some people grow up feeling they
have it made. Mom and Dad are so extremely accommodating that
these people have no cares during childhood. But you can see how this
lays the groundwork for later problems with worry when as adults,

their parents are not around to solve their problems. A worried panic can erupt over the slightest problem.

3. *A confused pattern.* Many adult worriers come from a childhood atmosphere that could be best described as confusing. They may grow up in a family where one or both parents is inconsistent in behavior because of alcoholism, temperament, or some other problem. Consequently, a feeling of confidence is never established in their lives, and worry is an outward manifestation of this background of turmoil.

4. *An alienating pattern.* Some problem worriers describe their developmental years as very lonely and devoid of satisfactory parental care. When the parents are frequently absent or are very passive, a person grows up being starved for proper guidance and direction. A feeling of insecurity can easily develop in such a situation, resulting in long-standing problems with worry.

We have examined only four developmental patterns, but you will notice that in each case some factor hinders the development of mature, independent thinking in the child. The circumstances may vary, but the result is the same: the tendency to excessive worry. Without the consistent teaching and encouragement needed to learn to tackle one's own problems, the individual grows into adulthood with an ego lacking in self-confidence.

In many cases, an adult who has persistent problems with worry can trace their origin to a family pattern that did not fully encourage proper objective thinking. In such a case the adult worrier may need help to rethink his foundation for personal stability and to focus mentally on new, confident patterns for problem-solving.

Letting Feelings Fester

Often worry can stem from festering irritations that have been inappropriately brushed aside. When we choose to ignore our feelings, they do not merely go away, rather, those feelings go underground, and can actually gain strength. A person who has problems with worry is often one who does not handle feelings of irritation at the proper moment.

Consider the mother who is uncomfortable about letting her pre-teen son stay out later at night than she would really like. Rather than responding to her initial feeling of discomfort and setting a comfortable time, she ignores the emotion and makes a decision against her best judgment. In doing so, she invites an evening of worry. Or, think about an employee who is upset by the way responsibilities have been assigned at the office. He feels cheated because he has been assigned a task that he knows little about. Rather than speak frankly about those feelings to the appropriate supervisor, he broods. Guess what happens next? Worry enters. By repressing his feeling of uneasiness, worry is the result.

Time and time again I talk with worriers who admit that they fall short in being able to share assertively their needs and feelings. Rather than seek open solutions to their inner frustrations, these worriers brood and allow problems to build. They try to live with a false assumption that if they ignore their problems they will go away. If worry is allowed to flourish, it only creates continuing heartaches. I have never met a problem worrier who consistently enjoyed life.

Case Study

Sheila was an attractive, middle-aged woman who said she had been through it all in terms of emotional turmoil. Through the years she had experienced problems with misguided anger, depression, envy, and other emotions, but foremost in her struggles had been a problem with chronic worry.

During her childhood, Sheila was considered to be above average in intelligence. This proved to be both a blessing and a curse, for while the advantages of being bright were obvious, the disadvantages were that the performance expectations of her parents and her teachers were heavy. Sheila was pushed to excel in her school work, in her musical abilities (she was an accomplished pianist), and in her Christian life. It was not enough for her to be average; she had to be better than her peers. You can imagine the tension this caused. While she worked hard to excel, she learned to fear mistakes. Sheila describes it as feeling that someone was constantly breathing down her neck, watching her every move. Yet in spite of this problem, she could usually be counted on to be efficient.

For years Sheila complied with the expectations set before her. She won musical contests. She excelled in school. She was apparently the perfect angel in her Christian walk. Throughout her entire childhood, she learned to stay ahead of the game by performing well. All the while, Sheila was subject to moments of nervousness, but she was skilled in hiding them.

However, her pattern of worry began to intensify during her adult years. In her early twenties, Sheila was easily frustrated by the ambiguities that came with dating. She persistently worried about being well received by her boyfriends. She worked hard to be socially adept, but doubt constantly plagued her. She married in her mid-twenties, but as she looks back on her decision to marry, she feels that it was made from a position of insecurity. She feared that another proposal might not come along.

Sheila describes her first fifteen years of marriage and family life as a total disaster. She says that she had been trained as a child to be so concerned with performance and outward appearances that she could hardly tolerate errors of any kind. She would come unglued when she and her husband had any disagreement. She created a near frenzy in her home, trying to make sure that her children behaved perfectly (which they didn't). Any chore she had to do around the house became so monumental that she created tension in herself and the entire family trying to do it flawlessly.

Sheila's social life was also unsatisfactory. She was extremely sensitive to the perceptions that others had of her. Consequently, she had problems with depression because she worried about her standing with friends and neighbors. Sheila hardly knew what it felt like to be calm and relaxed. She was too busy worrying about how she should behave in order to present herself with the most responsible, favorable image.

Fortunately, Sheila had the good sense to seek counseling for this problem. As we began to examine the build-up of worry in her life, Sheila began to pinpoint several problem areas. First, she realized that she had been so strictly trained that her efforts to be correct became a burden. She was able to see and admit that her self-confidence was quite fragile, hinging on her ability to follow an endless list of unspoken rules and regulations. In addition, she recognized that her worry persisted because she would not openly admit her feelings of insecurity, but let them fester inwardly. As she began honestly to examine her lifestyle, Sheila began to overhaul her family and social habits.

The first thing Sheila learned to do was to acknowledge her needs and her feelings in a calm, rational manner. She trained herself to take the intensity out of her voice and communicate her concerns in a way that her family and friends could receive without being threatened. As she was doing this, she noticed that she was taking herself less seriously, and this helped her to have a more balanced perspective on her thoughts and feelings.

Next, Sheila decided to take a long, hard look at her feelings of insecurity. She questioned herself daily about what it would take to make her feel secure. She quickly recognized that her security was on shaky ground when she depended totally on herself to be perfectly responsible. And she also recognized that she was asking for trouble when she concerned herself too much with the moods and emotions of others. As she pondered her need for security, a light clicked on in her mind. "Now I think I know why I've been told so many times to place my faith in God's love for me." She came to accept the idea that God loved her in spite of the rightness or wrongness of her ways. What a relief! She didn't have to be perfect!

Finally, it became clear to her that it was all right to share with family and friends how they could help make life easier for her; in fact, it was an act of responsibility. For so long she had been so concerned with trying to be perfect that she could not bear the thought of exposing her needs to anyone. But it was obvious that in repressing her needs, she was permitting feelings to build inside that erupted unpredictably. She was harming herself by playing the role of the martyr, overextending herself for the sake of avoiding friction.

In time, Sheila gained control over her pattern of worry. This emotion did sneak up on her from time to time, but it did not have the mastery it once had. By exploring her options and examining her inner thoughts, she learned that she could develop more calm, beneficial behavior patterns.

Controlling Worry

Admittedly, worry is not an easy emotion to control. By nature it is powerful and unpredictable. Yet, as Sheila discovered, individuals can examine their thought patterns and find ways to keep worry from being dominant.

Acknowledging God's Control

Persistent worriers are people trying to take matters into their own hands. The worrier assumes that one *should* be able to solve all problems. There is an unrealistic, humanistic assumption that the individual should be all powerful. Worry is a subtle way of trying to place human strength above God's strength.

To gain control over worry, we need to acknowledge that God is in charge of our lives. We have been given life by a loving God who is not going to allow us to fall upon circumstances that burden us beyond our capacity.

> Do not be anxious for your life, as to what you shall eat, or what you shall drink; nor for your body, as to what you shall put on. Is not life more than food, and the body than clothing? Look at the birds of the air, that they do not sow, neither do they reap, nor gather into barns, and yet your heavenly Father feeds them. Are you not worth more than they? . . . Therefore do not be anxious for tomorrow; for tomorrow will care for itself. Each day has enough trouble of its own (Matt. 6:25–26, 34).

In this famous teaching Jesus was emphasizing the fact that God takes care of His own. It is our job to live as best we can in a fashion that is pleasing to God. It is His delight to see that our efforts are rewarded. A person who is living for God need not concern himself with worries. To do so is to communicate a lack of faith in God's promise.

Years ago, Martin Luther said:

> I have one preacher that I love better than any other on earth; it is my little tame robin, who preaches to me daily. I put crumbs upon my windowsill, especially at night. He hops onto the windowsill when he wants his supply, and takes as much as he desires to satisfy his need.

From thence he always hops to a little tree close by and lifts up his voice to God and sings his carols of praise and gratitude, tucks his little head under his wing and goes fast to sleep, and leaves tomorrow to look after itself. He is the best preacher that I have on earth.

A Flexible Mindset

Once a person takes the first step to acknowledge that God is in control and knows what He is doing, it is possible to approach life with flexibility. To be flexible means that the individual is willing to adapt to people and circumstances without holding rigidly to set ways. It does not mean that the person drops all opinions and preferences, but rather that one's opinions and preferences are kept in perspective and do not generate worry.

Think of the flexibility exhibited by Jesus Christ. While He was a person who had very powerful opinions about the best ways to live responsibly, He did not insist that matters had to go His way before He could calmly relate to others, even when those others lived in ways that went totally against His beliefs. He didn't burden Himself with worry.

A man, once explained to me how he was able to incorporate flexibility into his life. "All my life I've had ideas about how I want people to behave and how situations should work out. But let's face it, in this world nothing is going to be that perfect. I could worry constantly about problems, but what good does it do me, or anyone else? Besides, I have better ways to expend my emotional energy. I want people to know that I love them, and I want to experience God's contentment in my life. If I worry about how things are not what I want them to be, I won't be able to enjoy other people or myself."

Worriers who hold rigidly to their rules and preferences are dangerously close to false pride. In a sense, they are saying, "Why can't life be the way I demand it to be?" In flexibility there is a sense of humbleness. It communicates, "I know what I want, and I'll do what I can be responsible, but I also recognize the imperfection of our sinful world. I'll let God handle the problems I can't."

Seeking the Positive

Worriers are pessimists. They assume the worst in trying circumstances. When a person gives himself over to a pattern of worry, he is assuming that the bottom is about to fall out. Usually when worry is dominant, the bottom does fall out.

"And we know that God causes all things to work together for good to

those who love God, to those who are called according to His purpose"
(Rom. 8:28). What does this mean? We are assured that in all circumstances, positive or negative, there is good to be found. Lessons can be
learned. Character can be built. This concept can be applied in some
very common situations:

A wife who has a very critical husband learns to love even when love
is not given in return.

A student who has three tests in one day is taught the value of
preparing ahead.

A parent who learns of a child's drug problem understands the
importance of forgiveness and unconditional love.

An employee who has more work than he can handle develops the art
of speaking up diplomatically for his needs.

A husband who has lost his sentimental love for his wife can find a
new appreciation for the love that continues as an act of the will.

A woman whose best friend has moved away can find the motivation
to place herself in new circles, creating new friendships.

No circumstance is so negative that a positive lesson cannot be
learned. I have found tremendous inspiration from reading Victor
Frankl, who shared his experience of living in a Jewish concentration
camp during World War II. In *Man's Search for Meaning*, Frankl
describes how he was stripped of all human dignity. His home and
family were taken from him. His head was shaved. His civilian clothes
were removed in favor of the demeaning striped suit given to the
prisoners. To shave, he daily had to find pieces of broken glass with
which to scrape his face. And yet through his miseries, Victor Frankl
developed a philosophy that would sustain him for the rest of his life.
He concluded that while his circumstances were indescribably despica-
ble, God had given him the inner strength to overcome whatever obstacles his captors placed in front of him. In fact, he concluded that by
living through this darkest period he would ever know, he was a better,
more mature individual.

We could all learn a great deal from Dr. Frankl's experience. If he
could call upon God to bring something positive out of his suffering, so
can we. No negative circumstance is so great that God cannot bring
about positive conclusions.

A Balanced Perspective

To have a balanced perspective is to understand the relative significance of an occurrence, to see objectively into the nature of a problem. A balanced perspective helps one sort out the essential from the trivial. It can give the insight needed to determine whether a problem can be effectively solved. Perspective could teach us that a problem is not solvable, in which case worry would be useless and a waste of energy. Perspective could also show us that constructive answers are available, and again, worry would be unnecessary. Energy could be better spent on the solutions.

And there are practical, everyday applications for a balanced perspective. A mother who has perspective on the milk spilt by her toddler can decide that picking up a sponge and calmly wiping up the mess is more productive than fretting and upsetting both herself and the child. The salesman who is late for an appointment can decide to think reasonably about his misfortune. He can determine to get to his destination safely and make the best use of his time once he gets there. A Christian who is aware of his sinful nature can scold himself for his failures, or he can learn to love himself in spite of his faults, just as God does.

A good perspective is not easy to achieve. Perhaps we can recite the right answers, but applying them is another story. Yet it is worth the effort.

Questions for Further Thought

Am I a responsible person? Is my sense of responsibility so strong that I fret when things do not go exactly like they are supposed to?

Do I allow fears to take charge of my emotions? When do I let irritations join with my fears?

How strong is my self-image? Have I allowed God's peace to reside in me?

When problems occur, do I focus on negatives? How can I become more solution-oriented?

What goals do I have in personal relations? How can I develop a solid sense of perspective regarding myself and the world around me?